Ultimate Book
of the
WORLD

The Ultimate Book of the WORLD

Clive Dickinson

RED FOX

A Red Fox Book
Published by Arrow Books Limited
20 Vauxhall Bridge Road, London SW1V 2SA

An imprint of the Random Century Group

London Melbourne Sydney Auckland
Johannesburg and agencies throughout the world

First published by Red Fox 1990

Set in Helvetica
by JH Graphics Ltd, Reading

Made and printed in Great Britain by
Courier International, Tiptree, Essex

ISBN 0 09 966310 4

Introduction

Did you know that the smallest country in the world has the lowest number of births? In fact, no one is born there at all!

Did you know that there's an island in the Pacific that exports bird droppings and another that makes most of its 'official' money from selling postage stamps?

Did you know that there's a town somewhere in Scandinavia called A and another further south in Europe called Y?

And do you know which is the first man-made object seen by astronauts as they return to earth from outer space?

If you don't know the answers to these questions, then it's just as well you've started reading *The Ultimate Book of the World*! Here you'll find all the up-to-date facts and figures about the world from Afghanistan to Zimbabwe, plus details about each country's history, weather, geography and people. And just in case you aren't sure where in the world to start looking for Tokelau or St Pierre and Miquelon, there's a brief regional description to help you out.

So dip inside and discover which worm is called the 'caviar of the Pacific', where Good King Wenceslas really lived, how many cars there are in the USA, which country has the longest coastline and where the largest eggs in the world have been found . . . and there are just a few facts about our amazing world to get you started!

Afghanistan

Official name: Republic of Afghanistan
History: Afghanistan was a kingdom until 1973 when the last king was deposed. The USSR sent troops to the country at the end of 1979 and fought a war against Afghan freedom fighters until 1989.
World location: Central Asia
Area: 647,497 km^2
Local time: 4½ hours ahead of GMT
Population: 15,510,000
Language: Pushtu and Dari (Persian)
Religion: Moslem
Capital: Kabul
Other major centres: Kandahar, Herat, Mazar-i-Sharif, Jalalabad
Money: Afghani = 100 puls
Weather: Dry with variation according to altitude. High areas like Kabul have very cold winters with heavy snowfalls. Lower areas have hot summers.
Main rivers: Helmand, Kabul and Oxus
Main mountain ranges: Hindu Kush, Koh-i-Baba, Band-i-Baian
National day: 27 April
National flag: Black, red and green horizontal stripes with the state emblem of a pulpit and niche in a mosque between two sheaves of corn surrounded by the sun's rays in the top left-hand corner.

- Although primary schools have been established throughout Afghanistan, secondary schools only exist in the major cities.
- Flat loaves of bread accompany most meals in Afghanistan. Afghans are fond of mutton and rice. Popular desserts include cheese, nuts, and fresh or dried fruits. Tea is a favourite drink.

Afghanistan

- In the early 1980s there were only about 12,000 television sets in the whole of Afghanistan, which averaged out at one set to every 1,400 people.
- Many Afghan men wear turbans made of strips of material that can be as long as 6 metres.
- There is only one railway line in Afghanistan, running for a distance of 200 km from the border with USSR to the industrial town of Pul-i-Khumri.

Albania

Official name: People's Socialist Republic of Albania
History: Albania was part of the Ottoman Empire centred in Turkey until 1912, when the country declared its independence. Italy invaded Albania in 1914 and again in 1939. In 1944 the country became a Communist republic.
World Location: South-east Europe. The Adriatic Sea lies to the west, Yugoslavia is to the north and east, and Greece to the south.
Area: 28,748 km^2
Local time: 1 hour ahead of GMT (summer time 2 hours ahead)
Population: 3,140,000
Language: Albanian
Religion: Religions are officially forbidden in Albania
Capital: Tirana
Other major centres: Durres, Shkoder, Elbasan
Money: Lek = 100 quintars
Weather: Mild, with wet winters and dry, hot summers on the coast; cooler and wetter inland
Main rivers: Semani, Drini, Vjosa
Main mountain ranges: Albanian Alps
National day: 11 January

National flag: Red, with a two-headed black eagle, above which is a red star with gold edges. The two-headed eagle was the symbol of a great Albanian hero named Skanderburg.

- Skanderburg ruled Albania during the 15th century. He was said to be enormously strong and according to legend once executed two criminals with one sword blow.
- Bread and dairy products like cheese and milk make up the daily diet of most Albanians.
- In Albania older students in full-time education also spend some of their time in military service or out at work.

Algeria

Official name: Democratic and Popular Republic of Algeria
History: Algeria was governed by France from the 19th century until 1962 when the country became independent.
World location: North-west Africa, with its northern coastline on the Mediterranean Sea
Area: 2,381,741 km²
Local time: 1 hour ahead of GMT
Population: 23,840,000
Language: Arabic, Berber, French
Religion: Moslem, with a small number of Christians, (mainly Roman Catholics)
Capital: Algiers
Other major centres: Oran, Annaba, Blida, Setif
Money: Algerian dinar = 100 centimes
Weather: Hot and dry in the south, cooler with greater rainfall on the coast

Algeria

Main river: Chéliff
Main mountain ranges: Atlas, Hoggar
National day: 1 November
National flag: Two vertical stripes of green and white, with a red crescent and a star in the centre.

- In Algeria, *mechoui* or baby lamb is a popular dish. Bedouins who make long journeys through the Sahara desert have traditionally enjoyed this dish roasted over a camp fire. In town and cities *mechoui* has been adapted to town life and the lamb is roasted in an oven. Algerians are fond of the type of bread eaten in France called *baguettes*, as well as the traditional flat bread eaten in the Arab world, known as *kesra*.
- The world's highest sand dunes are found in Algeria. These stand 430 metres high and stretch for 5 km from one 'wave crest' to the next.

Andorra

Official name: Co-principality of Andorra
History: Andorra has been governed by France and Spain since the 13th century.
World location: South-west Europe. Andorra is a tiny land-locked country in the Pyrenees, between France and Spain.
Area: 453 km²
Local time: 1 hour ahead of GMT (summer time 2 hours ahead)
Population: 50,000
Language: Catalan, also Spanish and French
Religion: Mainly Roman Catholic
Capital: Andorra la Vella
Other major centre: Les Escaldes

Money: Both French and Spanish currencies are used
Weather: Mild and dry with cool summers and cold winters
Main river: Valira
Main mountain range: Pyrenees
National day: 8 September
National flag: Three stripes of blue (representing France), gold (representing Spain) and red (in both French and Spanish flags). The stripes can be horizontal or vertical and sometimes the Andorran coat of arms or a little crown is set in the middle.

- Andorra is ruled jointly by the Spanish bishop of Urgel and the President of France. They are called the Princes of Andorra. Every second year the valleys of Andorra pay a tax of 960 francs to France and 460 pesetas to Spain.
- Andorra earns most of its money from tourism and over 6,000,000 people visit Andorra every year – that's 120 visitors for every person living in Andorra. If the same proportion of visitors came to the UK every year it would be like being visited by everybody on earth! In fact some of them would have to come twice to produce the correct total.

Angola

Official name: People's republic of Angola
History: Angola was a Portuguese colony for most of its history from the 15th century until 1975, when it became fully independent.
World location: West south Africa, bordering on the Atlantic Ocean
Area: 1,246,700 km^2

Angola

Local Time: 1 hour ahead of GMT
Population: 9,480,000
Language: Portuguese and many Bantu African languages. Spanish and French are also spoken.
Religion: The largest religious group practises traditional local religions. There are also some Roman Catholics and Protestants.
Capital: Luanda
Other major centres: Huambo, Lobito, Beneguela
Money: Kwanza = 100 lweis
Weather: Tropical in the north, sub-tropical in the south. There are two seasons: wet October to May, dry June to September.
Main rivers: Kunene, Kwanza, Zaire and Kwando
Main mountain ranges: Rand Plateau, Benguela Plateau, Bie Plateau
National day: 11 November
National flag: Red and black horizontal stripes, with gold star, half a gold cog wheel and a gold knife called a machete.

- During the 17th century between 5,000 and 10,000 people in Angola were captured and sent overseas to work as slaves in other countries.
- The *carnaval* ('festival' or 'carnival') is very popular in Angola and also very old. The better known carnivals that take place in Brazil were taken there by slaves sent from Angola.

Anguilla

History: British colony since the 17th century
World location: Eastern Caribbean Sea, in the Leeward Islands

Area: 91 km^2
Local time: 4 hours behind GMT
Population: 7,000
Language: English
Religion: Christian, mainly Protestant
Capital: The Valley
Money: East Caribbean dollar = 100 cents
Weather Sub-tropical, sunny and warm with almost constant sea breezes
National day: 30 May

- Anguilla is shaped rather like an eel and was probably given its name by Spanish explorers because of this.
- Caribbean cooking makes great use of sea food. Fish and shellfish are popular, especially the Caribbean lobster. Anguillans are also fond of kebabs – pieces of meat (usually beef on Anguilla) cooked and eaten on a skewer with pineapple and peppers.
- Anguilla has some of the finest white beaches in the Caribbean. The water is also very clear around the island, which makes it excellent for snorkelling and scuba diving.

Antigua and Barbuda

History: British colony since the 17th century, Antigua and Barbuda became independent 1 November 1981.
World location: Eastern Caribbean Sea, in the Leeward Islands
Area: 442 km^2
Local time: 4 hours behind GMT
Population: 80,000
Language: English

Antigua and Barbuda

Religion: Christian, mainly Protestant
Capital: St John's
Money: East Caribbean dollar = 100 cents
Weather: Sub-tropical, sunny and warm with almost constant sea breezes
National day: 1 November
National flag: Red, with an upside down triangle of (from top to bottom) black, blue and white. A golden sun is rising in the black area.

- In 1493 Christopher Columbus first discovered Antigua and named the island after a church in the Spanish city of Seville.
- The main foods eaten by the people of Antigua and Barbuda include beans, fish, lobsters and sweet potatoes. Tropical fruits are often eaten as dessert and the islanders make a special jam out of mangos.
- The West Indian cricketer Viv Richards represented Antigua and Barbuda in the 1988 West Indies touring side.
- Antigua was once the main British naval base in the Caribbean. It was from here that Admiral Nelson sailed to his great victory at the Battle of Trafalgar, fought off the coast of Spain close to Gibraltar in 1805. Unfortunately for Nelson it was also the battle in which he was killed.

Argentina

Official name: Argentine Republic
History: Spanish colony from the 16th century, Argentina became independent 1816.
World location: South-east of South America, with a long coastline on the South Atlantic.

Area: 2,776,889 km^2
Local time: 3 hours behind GMT
Population: 31,960,000
Language: Spanish
Religion: Christian, mainly Roman Catholic
Capital: Buenos Aires
Other major centres: Cordoba, Rosario, Mendoza, La Plata, San Miguel du Tucuman
Money: Austral = 100 centavos
Weather: Sub-tropical in the north to sub-arctic in the south
Main rivers: Parana, Negro, Salado
Main mountain ranges: Andes
National day: 25 May
National flag: Stripes of light blue top and bottom with a white stripe between them. A gold sun with a face is set in the middle of the white stripe.

- Argentina's name comes from the Latin word *argentum*, meaning 'silver'. The first Spanish explorers who went to Argentina in the 15th century gave it this name because they were searching for silver and gold.
- Argentina is famous for its meat. Beef, chicken and lamb are the most popular and Argentinians enjoy eating these over barbecues. One dish with a special Argentinian flavour is *asado con cuero*, beef roasted in its hide over an open fire. *Pucheras* (stews of chicken or other meats with vegetables) are popular and so are empanadas (pastries stuffed with meat, fruit, or seafood).
- Argentina may not be as well known as the Wild West of the USA, but it is just as much a cowboy country — in fact the earliest cowboys in America used Spanish techniques like those used in Argentina. The Argentinian cowboy is called a *gaucho*. Like American cowboys he wears a wide-brimmed hat but over the top half of his

body he wears a *poncho*, a blanket with a hole in the middle for his head.

- Argentinians have always been interested in horses. Some of the world's best polo players come from Argentina and the country is the home of the world's smallest breed of horses — the tiny Falabella which stands less than 76 cm high.

- One sport that originated in Argentina is a cross between polo and netball, called *pato*. When the game was first played in the 15th century it was very violent and cruel, but the modern game is played to strict rules between two teams of four riders. The aim of the game is to score goals by throwing a ball into an opponent's goal. To make it easy to handle on horseback the ball (the size of a small football) is fitted with six leather handles. Players have to carry it at arm's length to give their opponents a chance to snatch it away. Like polo, *pato* requires a good eye for a ball and good horsemanship.

- Buenos Aires is the largest city in the world south of the Equator.

Australia

Official name: Commonwealth of Australia
History: Former British colonies which became independent on 1 January, 1901
World location: South-west Pacific Ocean, occupying the whole continent of Australia
Area: 7,682,300 km^2
Local time: Because Australia is such a huge country it covers several time-zones. Western Australia is 8 hours ahead of GMT; Northern Territory 9½ hours ahead of GMT; Queensland 10 hours ahead of GMT; South

Australia 10½ hours ahead of GMT; Capital Territory, New South Wales, Victoria and Tasmania 11 hours ahead of GMT. (In eastern areas the time ahead of GMT is thirty minutes less from mid-March to the end of October.)

Population: 16,530,000
Language: English
Religion: Christian
Capital: Canberra
Other major centres: Sydney, Melbourne, Brisbane, Perth, Adelaide
Money: Australian dollar = 100 cents
Weather: Wide variation – tropical in the north, hot and dry in the centre, cooler in the south. The Snowy Mountains in the south-west have snow for half the year. (Countries, like Australia, in the southern hemisphere have their winter when we have summer and summer when we have winter.)
Main rivers: Murray-Darling, Flinders, Ashburton, Fitzroy
Main mountain ranges: Great Dividing Range, Macdonnel Ranges, Flinders Ranges, Australian Alps (including Snowy Mountains)
National day: 26 January
National flag: British Blue Ensign (blue flag with the Union Jack in the upper corner next to the flag pole). Below the Union Jack is a big star called the Commonwealth Star. There are also five small white stars representing the Southern Cross, a group of stars only seen south of the Equator.

- The original inhabitants of Australia, the Aborigines, are thought to have arrived from South-east Asia over 30,000 years ago.
- The Aborigines have many sacred sites in Australia, some of them decorated with paintings that are thousands of years old. Aborigines are famous for their

painting, though instead of using paper, they paint on the bark of the eucalyptus tree.

- The *woomera*, an Aboriginal throwing stick, can propel a spear a distance of over 120 metres.
- Water is scarce in Australia. The continent has the lowest annual rainfall of all the world's inhabited continents.
- Australia is the only country in the world that supports four types of football: Rugby Union, Rugby League, Soccer and Australian Rules Football.
- Meat forms an important part of the Australian diet. Beef is the most popular, followed by lamb, mutton, poultry and pork. Meat is usually grilled or roasted (barbecues are popular) and served with potatoes and other vegetables. Italian and Greek cooking has become popular in recent years as the number of immigrants from these countries has increased.
- The council in the town of Mt Isa in Western Queensland controls an area of 40,978 km², making it the world's largest town.
- The Nullarbor Plain in Southern Australia takes its name from two Latin words meaning 'no trees'. The railway line that crosses the Nullarbor runs in a straight line for 478 km in one section, making it the longest stretch of straight track in the world.

Austria

Official name: Republic of Austria

History: Originally part of the Austro-Hungarian Empire, the republic was created in 1918 after the First World War. Germany occupied Austria from 1938 to 1945. For the next ten years the country was controlled by the UK, USA, USSR and France, until Austria was made fully independent again in May 1955.

World location: Central Europe
Area: 83,855 km^2
Local time: 1 hour ahead of GMT (summer time 2
hours ahead)
Population: 7,600,000
Language: German; a few people speak Slovene and
Croatian
Religion: Christian, mainly Roman Catholic
Capital: Vienna
Other major centres: Graz, Linz, Salzburg, Innsbruck
Money: Schilling = 100 groschen
Weather: Very warm summers, cold winters with heavy
snowfall especially in the mountains
Main rivers: Danube, Inn, Mur
Main mountain range: Alps
National day: 26 October
National flag: Three horizontal stripes of red, white, red.
This is one of the oldest national flags in the world.
According to tradition it came into being in the late 12th
century when Leopold of Austria was badly wounded in
a battle fought in 1191. When he removed his tunic, it
was stained red with blood, all except for a band round
the middle where his belt had been. Seeing this,
Leopold decreed that thereafter Austria should have a
red flag with a white band across its middle.

- Some of the festivals celebrated in Austria date back to
  before Christian times. At the beginning of spring people
  in many areas still perform an ancient rite to chase away
  evil spirits. They wear special masks to frighten the
  spirits away and walk through the streets waving large
  sticks to scare them off.
- Austria is a country where sausages have always been
  popular, either cooked or eaten cold as salamis. One of
  the most famous Austrian dishes is *weiner schnitzel*, a
  cutlet of veal cooked in breadcrumbs. Side dishes

include dumplings, noodles and potatoes. Cakes and pastries made by Austrian bakers are world famous.

- In a country famous for its good food, it's curious that the world record for a human being surviving without food or water is held by an Austrian. His name was Andreas Mihavecz and he survived for eighteen days.
- Over four-tenths of Austria is covered by forest.

Bahamas

Official name: The Commonwealth of the Bahamas
History: The Bahamas were discovered by the Spanish expedition led by Christopher Columbus in 1492 (San Salvador was the first place he landed in the New World.) Britain controlled the islands for most of their history from the 17th century until they became independent in 1973
World location: Western Atlantic Ocean. The Bahamas are a chain of 700 islands lying west of Cuba.
Area: 13,939 km^2
Local time: 5 hours behind GMT (summer time 4 hours behind)
Population: 240,000
Language: English
Religion: Christian
Capital: Nassau
Other major centre: Freeport
Money: Bahamian dollar = 100 cents
Weather: Warm and comfortable throughout the year. Rain falls mainly in May-June and September-October.
National day: 10 July
National flag: Three horizontal bands of blue (representing the sea), yellow (for the islands' sandy

beaches) and blue. Next to the flagpole is a black triangle, a symbol of national unity.

- Many of the Bahamas' most important exports come from the sea. The islands send turtle shell, conch shell and sponges to markets all round the world.
- *Callaloo*, one of the best known soups in Caribbean cooking, is a great favourite in the Bahamas. It's made from taro-leaf, crab meat and the vegetable okra. Other dishes eaten in the Bahamas are roast suckling pig, stuffed crab and banana desserts.

Bahrain

Official name: State of Bahrain
History: Bahrain was first ruled by a sheik. In 1882 it came under British protection until full independence in 1971.
World location: Middle East. Bahrain is a chain of 33 small islands in the Persian Gulf between the Qatar peninsula and the north-eastern coast of Saudi Arabia.
Area: 622 km²
Local time: 3 hours ahead of GMT
Population: 480,000
Language: Arabic
Religion: Moslem
Capital: Manama
Other major centre: Muharraq
Money: Bahrain dinar = 1000 fils
Weather: Hot and humid in summer, otherwise warm and pleasant
National day: 16 December
National flag: Red, with a white band with a jagged edge like a saw blade next to the flag pole.

Bahrain

- *Bahrain* is an Arabic word meaning 'two seas'
- When oil was first discovered in Bahrain in 1932 it became the first oil-rich state in the Persian Gulf.
- Herbs and spices play an important part in Arab cooking. Among the chief foods eaten in Bahrain are dates, fish, fruit and rice. One of the Bahrainian specialities is a dish called *kofta wa kebab*, which consists of chunks of lamb and minced meat placed on a skewer and grilled.

Bangladesh

Official name: People's Republic of Bangladesh
History: Originally part of British India, the country became the eastern part of Pakistan in 1947. Bangladesh became independent in 1971
World location: South Asia, east of India, bordering on the north of the Bay of Bengal
Area: 143,998 km^2
Local time: 6 hours ahead of GMT
Population: 104,530,000
Language: Bangla (Bengali); many people speak English
Religion: Mainly Moslem
Capital: Dhaka
Other major centres: Chittagong, Khulna, Rajshai
Money: Taka = 100 poisha
Weather: Tropical, hot and humid with very heavy rain in the monsoon season
Main rivers: Ganges, Brahmaputra, Jumna, Meghna
National day: 26 March
National flag: Green with a red disc.

- The heaviest hailstones ever recorded fell on

Bangladesh on 14 April 1986. They are said to have weighed 1.02 kg and according to reports they killed ninety-two people.

- Eight out of ten people who work in Bangladesh work on the land.
- Bangladesh is the world's leading producer of jute, the coarse material that is used for making ropes and canvas. The great rivers that flood the country so often also make it very fertile, and Bangladesh is the world's third largest grower of rice.
- Rice and fish are the two most important foods eaten in Bangladesh. Both are usually served in a spicy curry sauce.
- The delicate form of embroidered quilting known as *Kantha* has been practised in Bangladesh for hundreds of years since the days of the great Moghul emperors of India, and is still being made today.

Barbados

History: British colony from the 17th century, Barbados became independent in 1966.
World location: Eastern Caribbean Sea. Barbados is the most easterly of the Caribbean islands.
Area: 430 km²
Local time: 4 hours behind GMT
Population: 250,000
Language: English
Religion: Christian
Capital: Bridgetown
Other major centre: Speightstown
Money: Barbados dollar = 100 cents
Weather: Humid in the wet season June – November, otherwise warm and comfortable

Barbados

National day: 30 November
National flag: Three vertical stripes of blue, yellow and blue. In the centre of the yellow stripe is a black, three-pointed spear called a trident.

- Almost half the population of Barbados live in or around Bridgetown. The city is not only the principal port, it is also the main business centre in the Caribbean.
- Anyone visiting Barbados should try *Jug-jug*, a type of meat pudding made with grain and peas. Other popular foods are fish and shellfish, and tropical fruits like coconut and mango.
- Most of the fish caught off Barbados are flying fish.
- At the end of the sugar cane harvest each year the people of Barbados celebrate Crop Over, a form of harvest festival with steel bands and colourful costumes.

Belgium

Official name: Kingdom of Belgium
History: Part of the Netherlands from 1815, Belgium became independent in 1830. Germany occupied the country during both World Wars.
World location: Western Europe, bordering the North Sea
Area: 30,519 km^2
Local time: 1 hour ahead of GMT (summer time 2 hours ahead)
Population: 9,920,000
Language: Dutch (Flemish) and French
Religion: Christian, mainly Roman Catholic with some Protestants
Capital: Brussels
Other major centres: Antwerp, Ghent, Charleroi, Liège

Money: Belgian franc = 100 centimes
Weather: Mild winters and cool summers
Main rivers: Schelde, Meuse
Main mountain range: Ardennes
National day: 21 July
National flag: Three vertical stripes of black, yellow and red.

- Pigeon-racing is said to have started in Belgium, developing from the use of pigeons to carry messages.
- It was a Belgian named Jean Merlin who invented roller skates in 1760.
- Belgians are fond of fish, particularly eels, cockles and mussels. Two dishes that have made Belgian cooking famous are *carbonade* (beef stewed in beer) and *water-zooi* (a delicious stew made of chicken or fish).

Belize

History: British colony from the 18th century, Belize became independent in 1981.
World location: Central America, bordering the Caribbean Sea
Area: 22,965 km²
Local time: 6 hours behind GMT
Population: 170,000
Language: English, Spanish
Religion: Christian, mainly Roman Catholic
Capital: Belmopan
Other major centre: Belize City
Money: Belizean dollar = 100 cents
Weather: Sub-tropical with little variation in temperature and high rainfall
Main rivers: Hondo, Belize

Belize

Main mountain range: Maya Mountains
National day: 21 September
National flag: Blue, with red bands top and bottom. In the centre is a white disc with the coat of arms of Belize surrounded by a green garland.

- The ancient Maya civilization of Central America existed in Belize many centuries before the birth of Jesus Christ. It reached its peak in about the 8th century AD, but in all those hundreds of years the Mayas never discovered or made use of the wheel. There are still descendants of the Mayas living in Belize today.
- Belize is named after the words in the Mayan language meaning 'muddy water'.
- Almost eighty per cent of Belize is covered by forests and mahogany grown in them is one of the country's main exports.
- Fish forms an important part of Belizean cooking. There's one popular dish called *codfish holiday*, made from cod and vegetables, and another delicacy known as *Soupa de Hess*, which is a soup made from conch, a type of shellfish whose shells are almost more famous than the fish itself.

Benin

Official name: People's republic of Benin
History: Formerly a province of French West Africa, Benin became fully independent in 1960.
World location: West Africa. Benin runs north from a strip of coast on the Atlantic Ocean.
Area: 112,622 km^2
Local time: 1 hour ahead of GMT
Population: 4,450,000

Language: French is the official language; local languages, principally Fon, are also spoken.
Religion: Traditional local religions have the most followers. Just under a quarter of the people are Christian (mainly Roman Catholic).
Capital: Porto-Novo
Other major centres: Cotonou, Parakou, Abomey
Money: CFA franc = 100 centimes
Weather: Hot and dry in the north, tropical nearer the coast with rain from March to July and from October to November
Main rivers: Ouémé, Niger
National day: 30 November
National flag: Green with a five-pointed star in the upper corner nearest the flagpole.

- Early in the 19th century Benin was a powerful African kingdom famous for its skill in working with bronze and also for women warriors who fought in its army.
- Benin gives its name to a large bay called the Bight of Benin, which was feared by early sailors. The Bight of Benin was so hazardous that a rhyme was made up warning seafarers about it. It goes:

> Beware, beware the Bight of Benin,
> For few come out, though many go in.

- For a long time drums were used to communicate between one village and another in Benin. The very biggest drums were up to two metres long.
- As in many poor countries, the people of Benin have little chance of going to school and as recently as ten years ago fewer than three people in ten could read or write.

Bhutan

Official name: Kingdom of Bhutan
History: Under British protection from the 18th century, Bhutan came under Indian protection in 1949.
World location: Central Asia. Bhutan is a small mountainous country in the eastern Himalayas.
Area: 47,000 km^2
Local time: 6 hours ahead of GMT
Population: 1,450,000
Language: Dzongkha (a form of Tibetan) is the official language. English is also spoken by government officials.
Religion: Mainly Buddhist. A quarter of the population are Hindus.
Capital: Thimphu
Money: Ngultrum = 100 chetrums
Weather: Varies with altitude: the south sub-tropical with heavy rainfall, the mountains of the north cold with snow on the summits all year round
Main rivers: Amo-Chu, Wang-chu, Machu
Main mountain range: Himalayas
National day: 17 December
National flag: Yellow and orange divided diagonally, with a white dragon in the centre.

- Bhutan is not a good country to be in if you happen to be in a hurry to use the telephone. They have only recently been installed in Bhutan and five years ago there was still only one telephone to every 720 people in the country.
- The postal service in Bhutan is less than thirty years old too.

Bolivia

Official name: Republic of Bolivia
History: A former Spanish colony Bolivia became independent in 1825.
World location: West central South America
Area: 1,098,581 km²
Local time: 4 hours behind GMT
Population: 6,990,000
Language: Spanish is the official language. Indian languages like Quechu and Aymara are also spoken by many people.
Religion: Christian, mainly Roman Catholic
Capital: Sucre. La Paz is the seat of government.
Other major centres: Santa Cruz, Cochabamba, Oruro
Money: Boloiviano = 100 centavos
Weather: Varies with altitude: the low-lying areas of the Amazon Basin are warm and damp all year round; the highland areas around La Paz have clear, dry weather from May to November, but nights are cold in June and July.
Main rivers: Beni, Mamore, Pilcomayo, Paraguay
Main mountain range: Andes
National day: 6 August
National flag: Three horizontal stripes of red, yellow and green, with the national emblem in the centre.

- Bolivia has the highest railway station in the world. Anyone catching a train to Condor, high in the Andes mountains, will get out on to the platform at a height of 4,786 metres above sea level.
- La Paz is the highest capital in the world at 3,684 metres above sea level.
- The border between Bolivia and Peru runs through Lake Titicaca, the largest lake in South America. 3,800 metres above sea level, it is the highest lake in the world. Small

steamships built in the UK and carried up to the lake from the coast of Peru still sail between the two countries.

- Potatoes have always played an important part in the Bolivian diet. A dried form of potato, called *chuno*, is often cooked in stews.
- Since independence Bolivia has seen a lot of political changes with no period of really stable government. Since 1966 alone there have been fifteen presidents.

Botswana

Official name: The Republic of Botswana
History: Under British protection from 1885, Botswana became independent in 1966
World location: South Central Africa
Area: 582,000 km²
Local time: 2 hours ahead of GMT
Population: 1,210,000
Language: English is the official language, Setswana the national language.
Religion: Christian. Traditional local religions are also practised.
Capital: Gaborone
Other major centres: Francistown, Selibi-Phikwe
Money: Pula = 100 thebe
Weather: Sub-tropical with dry desert areas in the south and west
Main rivers: Chobe, Shashi
National day: 30 September
National flag: Light blue, with black stripe edged in white.

- The empty shells of ostrich eggs are used to store water in parts of Botswana.

- The *mophane* worm is collected for food in Botswana. In fact it has become such a delicacy that worms have recently been canned and sold to other countries.
- The Kalahari Christmas Tree is found throughout Botswana. Its wood is very hard and used for making walking sticks and spear handles. The leaves and bark are also effective in curing skin infections.
- A great deal of the land in Botswana is dry scrubland. Water is very scarce throughout the country and in eighty per cent of Botswana there is no surface water. All the water used has to be drawn from wells or boreholes in the ground.

Brazil

Official name: Federative Republic of Brazil
History: A Portuguese colony from 1500, Brazil became independent in 1822 and a republic in 1889.
World location: Central and east South America, bordering the South Atlantic Ocean. Brazil is the fifth largest country on earth.
Area: 8,511,965 km²
Local time: Brazil stretches over four time zones: Fernando do Noronha 1 hour behind GMT; East 2 hours behind GMT; West 3 hours behind GMT; State of Acre 4 hours behind GMT. (From February to October these times are one further hour behind GMT.)
Population: 144,430,000
Language: Portuguese
Religion: Christian (mainly Roman Catholic)
Capital: Brasilia
Other major centres: Sao Paolo, Rio de Janeiro, Salvador, Belo Horizonte, Recife, Porto Alegre
Money: Cruzado = 100 centavos

Brazil

Weather: Mainly tropical. Colder in the south and east. Warm and humid in the Amazon Basin

Main rivers: Amazon, Parana, Sao Franscisco

Main mountain ranges: Serra do Mor, Serra Geral, Serra de Mantiqueira

National day: 7 September

National flag: Green, with yellow diamond in the centre of which is a blue globe with stars and a white band carrying the motto *Ordem e Progressio* ('Order and Progress'). The green and yellow represent Brazil's forests and the country's minerals.

- Brazil occupies almost half the area of South America and nearly half the continent's people live in the country.
- Four out of ten of the people in Brazil are under fifteen years old.
- Brazil is the only Portuguese-speaking nation in Latin America.
- Rio de Janeiro has the world's largest football stadium, the Maracana Municipal stadium, which can hold 205,000 people.
- The Guaira falls that lie on the border between Brazil and Paraguay can reach a maximum rate of flow of 50,000 cubic metres per second in the rainy season, making them the greatest falls in the world during that period.
- The Amazon has the greatest flow of fresh water in the world. When it is in flood the river can discharge over 200,000 m^3 of water per second into the Atlantic Ocean and the silt brought down by the Amazon can still be seen almost 200 km out to sea.
- Brasilia has the world's widest road, the Monumental Axis, which is 250 metres wide and 2.4 km long.
- At first rubber trees only grew in the forests of the Amazon basin. In the late 19th century rubber seeds were shipped to Kew Gardens in London where they grew into trees. From there rubber trees were sent to Malaysia to begin the great rubber plantations in that country.

● Brazil is known as the world's largest 'coffee pot'. Every year the country produces about a quarter of the world's coffee.

Brunei

Official name: Brunei Darussalam
History: Brunei was a powerful state in the 16th century. It came under British protection in the 19th century and became fully independent in 1984.
World location: South-east Asia. Brunei is on the north-west coast of the island of Borneo.
Area: 5,765 km^2
Local time: 8 hours ahead of GMT
Population: 240,000
Language: Malay, Chinese
Religion: Mainly Moslem, with some Buddhists and Christians
Capital: Bandar Seri Begawan
Money: Brunei dollar = 100 sen
Weather: Tropical, hot and humid, with cool nights
Main river: Brunei River
National day: 23 February
National flag: Yellow, with stripes of white and black running diagonally from the upper corner by the flagpole. On the stripes is the national emblem in red – a tower with wings on top, surrounded by a crescent with two hands pointing upwards on either side. Beneath the crescent is the motto 'Always serve with the guidance of God'.

● Part of Bandar Seri Begawan is built on piles (heavy beams driven into the ground), which make many of the buildings look as if they are standing on stilts.

Bulgaria

Official name: People's Republic of Bulgaria
History: Ruled by Turkey from the 15th century, Bulgaria became independent in 1908; Bulgaria introduced reforms into its Communist government in 1989.
World location: South-east Europe, with its eastern coastline on the Black Sea
Area: 110,912 km^2
Local time: 2 hours ahead of GMT (summer time 3 hours ahead)
Population: 8,990,000
Language: Bulgarian
Religion: Christian, mainly Eastern Orthodox; Moslem
Capital: Sofia
Other major centres: Plovdiv, Varna, Ruse
Money: Lev = 100 stotinki
Weather: Hot, dry summers and mild, damp winters in the south. Further north the winters are colder with greater rainfall in summer and autumn.
Main rivers: Danube, Iskar, Maritsa
Main mountain range: Balkan Mountains
National day: 9 September
National flag: Three horizontal stripes of white, red and green. In the upper corner nearest the flagpole is the symbol of Bulgaria, a lion enclosed by two sheaves of corn above which is a red star.

- In central Bulgaria is a valley called the Valley of the Roses, which has the world's largest rose gardens. The flowers grown here produce attar of roses, an oil used in perfumes. Bulgaria produces eighty per cent of the world's attar of roses.
- Bulgaria specializes in making breads from butter, cheese and yoghurt. Many people claim that Bulgarian

yoghurt is the best in the world, and the Bulgarians certainly think that it helps them to live to a good old age.

- Puppets are a popular form of entertainment in Bulgaria and the country had nineteen puppet theatres in 1985.

Burkina Faso

History: Formerly a province of French West Africa, Upper Volta, as the country was then called, became independent in 1960. The name was changed to Burkina Faso in 1984.
World location: West Africa
Area: 274,200 km²
Local time: GMT
Population: 8,510,00
Language: French is the official language. Local languages are also spoken
Religion: Traditional local religions have the greatest number of followers. There are slightly fewer Moslems and a small number of Christians.
Capital: Ouagadougou
Other major centres: Bobo-Dioulasso, Koudougou
Money: CFA franc = 100 centimes
Weather: Tropical; dry from December to April, wetter from May to November
Main rivers: Black Volta, Red Volta and White Volta
National day: 4 August
National flag: Three horizontal stripes representing the three main rivers: black, white and red.

- The three rivers of Burkina Faso produce an annual catch amounting to 7,000 tonnes of fish.
- As recently as 1980 there was just one doctor to every 46,250 people in Burkina Faso.

Burma (Myanmar)

Official name: Union of Myanmar
History: Burma was part of British India until it became independent in 1948. In 1989 it changed its name to Myanmar.
World location: East Asia, with its western coastline on the Bay of Bengal
Area: 676,552 km²
Local Time: 6½ hours ahead of GMT
Population: 39,970,000
Language: Burmese is the official language. English is still used by many people.
Religion: Mainly Buddhist
Capital: Rangoon (Yangoon)
Other major centres: Mandalay, Moulmein, Pegu
Money: Kyat = 100 pyas
Weather: Tropical monsoon in the interior, drier and more humid in the north
Main rivers: Irrawaddy, Salween, Sittang, Mekong
Main mountain ranges: Arakan Yoma, Pegun Yoma
National day: 4 January
National flag: Red, with blue panel in upper corner nearest the flagpole. On the blue is a circle of fourteen stars within which is a cogwheel and ears of rice.

- As the Burmese flag suggests, rice is the country's principal food. Many Burmese dishes are seasoned with curry powder, one popular example being *panthay khowse* (noodles and chicken). Many people in Burma chew betel nut in the same way that those in the western world chew gum.
- The women of the Padaung or Koreni tribe follow the custom of fitting copper coils around their necks to make them longer. The greatest extent to which a neck has been stretched over many years is 40 cm.

- A former king of Burma named Minhti is said to have had one of the longest reigns in history. During the late 13th and 14th centuries Minhti reigned for ninety-five years.
- Some bamboos in the forests of Burma have been recorded growing at the rate of nearly one metre a day.
- For centuries the rivers of Burma provided the main means of travelling around the country. Today the Irrawaddy is navigable for nearly 1500 km inland and the Chindwin for over 600m.
- Although Burma has almost 4,500 km of railway track, it has no international rail connections with any of its neighbouring countries.

Burundi

Official name: Republic of Burundi
History: Burundi was a kingdom ruled by Mwamis from the 16th century. It was occupied by Germany at the end of the 19th century. From 1919 it was controlled by Belgium and became independent in 1962.
World location: Central Africa
Area: 27,834 km^2
Local time: 2 hours ahead of GMT
Population: 5,150,000
Language: Kirundi; French is also an official language
Religion: Mainly Christian, with a small number of Moslems and followers of traditional local religions
Capital: Bujumbura
Other major centre: Gitega
Money: Burundi franc = 100 centimes
Weather: Hot and humid in the lowlands; the highlands are cooler

Burundi

Main rivers: Kagera, Ruzizi
National day: 1 July
National flag: White cross with a white disc at the centre. In the cross are three red stars. The areas above and below the cross are red; those on each side are green.

- Music is an important part of life in Burundi. Popular musical instruments are the *inanga* (harp) and the *dingidi* (a fiddle with one string).
- In 1983 there was one television set to every 17,840 people in Burundi and a year later the figures for cars showed that there was one car for every 609 people in the country.

Cambodia

Official name: State of Cambodia
History: Between the 10th and 14th centuries Kampuchea was the centre of the powerful Khmer Empire. In the 19th century Cambodia came under French protection. It became a fully independent kingdom in 1955, but the king was deposed in 1970, a civil war followed and the country was invaded by Vietnam in 1978. The Vietnamese forces withdrew in 1989 and further fighting broke out.
World location: South-east Asia, with its coastline on the Gulf of Siam.
Area: 181,035 km^2
Local time: 7 hours ahead of GMT
Population: 7,870,000
Language: Khmer (Cambodian) is the official language.
Religion: Mainly Buddhism
Capital: Phnom Penh

Other major centres: Kompong Cham, Battambang
Money: Riel = 100 sen
Weather: Tropical, high temperatures all year round
Main river: Mekong
Main mountain range: Chaine des Cardamomes
National day: 17 April
National flag: Red, with a five-towered silhouette of the famous temple of Ankor Wat in the centre in yellow.

- There are seventy-two letters in the alphabet used in Cambodia, making it the longest in the world and two and three-quarters times the length of the English alphabet.

Cameroon

Official name: Republic of Cameroon
History: Formerly a French colony, Cameroon was divided into Fench and British territories in 1919. Following independence in 1960 and 1961, the two joined as a republic in 1972.
World location: West central Africa
Area: 475,442 km²
Local time: 1 hour ahead of GMT
Population: 10,670,000
Language: French and English are the official languages; local Bantu languages are also spoken.
Religion: Almost equal numbers of Christians and followers of traditional local religions, with a small number of Moslems
Capital: Yaoundé
Other major centres: Nkongsamba, Kumba
Money: CFA franc = 100 centimes

Cameroon

Weather: Hot and rainy in the coastal areas; cooler and drier inland
Main rivers: Sanaga, Nyong
Main mountain range: Massif de Ladamaoua
National day: 20 May
National flag: Vertical stripes of green, red and yellow, with a yellow star on the red stripe.

- Cameroon was mentioned in the writings of the ancient explorer, Hanno the Carthaginian, who lived in the 6th century BC. He described Mount Cameroon as the *Chariot of the Gods*.
- Cameroon is the only country in Africa that has both French and English as its official languages.
- More than twenty times the amount of rain falls on the coastal areas of Cameroon as falls on the dry northern areas near Lake Chad.

Canada

Official name: Dominion of Canada
History: Former British provinces in North America which became independent in 1867
World location: Northern half of North America. Canada is the second largest country in the world.
Area: 9,976,139 km²
Local time: Due to its size Canada covers several time zones: Newfoundland 3½ hours behind GMT; Atlantic Time 4 hours behind GMT; Eastern Time 5 hours behind GMT; Central Time 6 hours behind GMT; Mountain Time 7 hours behind GMT; Pacific Time 8 hours behind GMT. (In summer these times are 1 hour less behind GMT.)
Population: 25,950,000
Language: English and French

Religion: Christian
Capital: Ottawa
Other major centres: Toronto, Montreal, Vancouver, Ottawa-Hull, Edmonton, Calgary, Winnipeg, Quebec
Money: Canadian dollar = 100 cents
Weather: Great extremes. The north is very cold. The Pacific coast and south are milder in summer, but winters are very cold in the central areas.
Main rivers: Mackenzie, Yukon, St Lawrence, Nelson
Main mountain ranges: Rocky Mountains, Coast Mountains, Mackenzie Mountains
National day: 1 July
National flag: Red maple leaf on a white square, with vertical red stripes on either side.

- Indians and the Innuit (Eskimos) were the first inhabitants of Canada. Today there are about 23,000 Innuit living in Canada. *Innuit* means 'the people' in their language.
- Nearly one-third of Canadians are French-speaking.
- Canada is the world's leading exporter of fish. Salt and fresh-water fish together earn over £350 million for Canada each year.
- The Atlantic giant squid, found off the east coast of Canada, has the largest eye of any known animal, either living or extinct.
- Canadian cooking reflects influences from France and the USA. Early French settlers left many of their recipes for later generations of Canadians; one traditionally served on Christmas Eve is *tourtière* (pork pie). Steaks, beans and pancakes are popular American dishes that Canadians also enjoy today.
- Canada has the world's longest coastline, measuring 250,000 km. Its border with the USA is also the world's longest continuous frontier, stretching to 6,416 km.
- The world's longest oil pipeline begins in Canada and ends just across the border in the USA. From Edmonton

in the Canadian province of Alberta the pipeline runs for a distance of 2,856 km to Buffalo in New York State.

- Canada's Lake Superior, one of the Great Lakes of North America, is the world's largest freshwater lake, with an area of 82,350 km^2, almost four times the size of Wales.

- In 1796 the first stretch of Yonge Street running from Toronto was completed. Even then it was a long street, running almost fifty-six km. However, Yonge Street has been extended in the last 200 years and a drive down it now would take you almost 1,900 km from Toronto to Rainy River on the US border.

Cape Verde

Official name: Republic Cape Verde
History: A Portuguese colony from the 15th century, Cape Verde gained full independence in 1975.
World location: Eastern Atlantic Ocean. Cape Verde consists of fifteen small islands 600 km west of the coast of Senegal, in West Africa.
Area: 4,033 km^2
Local time: 1 hour behind GMT
Population: 360,000
Language: Portuguese is the official language, though most people also speak Crioulo
Religion: Christian (Roman Catholic)
Capital: Praia
Other major centre: Mindelo
Money: Cape Verde escudo = 100 centavos
Weather: Hot and dry, cooled by sea breezes
National day: 5 July
National flag: Vertical red stripe next to the flagpole, with horizontal stripes of yellow and green beside it.

- Very little rain has fallen on Cape Verde during the last ten years. As a result the country depends on food aid from other nations and many people are leaving to live in other countries, principally Portugal, Senegal and the USA.
- Fishermen from Cape Verde catch 200 tonnes of lobsters every year.
- Less than one-third of the roads in Cape Verde are paved. The others have loose gravel surfaces.
- In 1981 fewer than half of the people in Cape Verde could read and write.

Cayman Islands

Official name: Colony of the Cayman Islands
History: A British colony since the 17th century
World location: Caribbean Sea. The Cayman Islands lie 300 km south of Cuba.
Area: 259 km²
Local time: 5 hours behind GMT
Population: 23,400
Language: English
Religion: Christian
Capital: Georgetown
Money: Cayman Islands dollar = 100 cents
Weather: Tropical, with a cool season from November to March
National flag: British blue ensign, with the badge of the Cayman Islands.

- When Christopher Columbus first discovered the Cayman Islands he named them *Las Tortugas*, meaning 'The Turtles' in Spanish, because of the great number of turtles living on the islands. Today there is a farm on the

Cayman Islands which rears turtles. Many different types of turtle are found on the islands and some of the endangered species, like the Green Turtle, are bred here to prevent them becoming extinct.

- Making jewellery from black coral has developed into a profitable industry in the Cayman Islands. Unfortunately supplies of local coral are getting smaller and imported coral now has to be used.

- The traditional boat in the Cayman Islands is the Cat-boat, which is used for sailing and fishing. It is so easy to manoeuvre that it is said to be able to 'turn on a sixpence'.

- The Cayman islands are an important financial centre and there is approximately one bank or trust company to every forty-six people.

Central African Republic

History: One of four territories in French Equatorial Africa, the Central African Republic became independent in 1960.
World location: Central Africa
Area: 622,984 km²
Local time: 1 hour behind GMT
Population: 2,770,000
Language: French is the official language.
Religion: Over half the population follow traditional local religions; there are smaller numbers of Roman Catholics, Protestants and Moslems.
Capital: Bangul
Other major centres: Bambari, Bouar
Money: CFA franc = 100 centimes
Weather: Hot and humid with heavy rainfall from June to October in the forest areas of the south-west

Main river: Oubangui
National day: 1 December
National flag: Four horizontal stripes of blue, white, green and yellow, with a vertical stripe of red in the middle. There is a yellow star in the upper corner nearest the flagpole.

- The Central African Republic is one of the world's poorest countries. Ironically almost a quarter of its export earnings come from diamonds, some of the world's most expensive gems.
- Almost nine out of every ten people who work in the Central African Republic are employed in growing food to feed the country's population. That leaves only one person in ten to do all the other work, including that which earns money from other countries.

Chad

Official name: Republic of Chad
History: Chad used to be another of the territories that made up French Equatorial Africa. It achieved full independence in 1960.
World location: Central Africa
Area: 1,284,000 km²
Local time: 1 hour ahead of GMT
Population: 5,400,000
Language: French is the official language, but over 100 local languages are also spoken. In the desert areas of the north Arabic is spoken by many people.
Religion: Northern and Central Chad is chiefly Moslem. In the south the largest religious group practises traditional local religions; there are also a smaller number of Christians.

Chad

Capital: N'Djaména
Other major centres: Sarh, Moundou, Abéché
Money: CFA franc = 100 centimes
Weather: The northern desert areas are very hot and dry. The south is milder and very wet.
Main rivers: Chari, Bahr Kéita
Main mountain ranges: Tibesti, Ennedi
National day: 13 April
National flag: Three vertical stripes of blue, yellow and red.

- Lake Chad is considerably smaller today than when it was first discovered by Europeans during the 19th century. It is all that is left of an inland sea that once existed in this part of the Sahara desert.
- Rock engravings found in Chad and dating from 900 BC show elephants, rhinoceroses and hippopotami, which roamed the thick vegetation that once grew in what is now the world's largest desert.

Chile

Official name: Republic of Chile
History: A Spanish colony from the 16th century, Chile became independent in 1818.
World location: South-West of South America. Chile has a long coastline on the Pacific Ocean
Area: 756,945 km²
Local time: 3 hours behind GMT
Population: 12,750,000
Language: Spanish
Religion: Christian (Roman Catholic)
Capital: Santiago

Other major centres: Viña del Mar, Talcahuano, Chillan, Arica
Money: Chilean peso = 100 centavos
Weather: Tropical in the north, very cold in the far south and in the mountains
Main rivers: Loa, Maule, Bio Bio
Main mountain range: Andes
National day: 18 September
National flag: Two horizontal stripes of white and red. In the upper corner nearest the flagpole is a blue square with a white star.

- The Atacama Desert in Chile suffered the longest drought ever recorded, nearly 400 years between one rain shower and the next.
- Chile's national dance is called the *cueca*. It is accompanied by the guitar while the dancers swing large handkerchiefs.
- With such a long coastline on the Pacific Ocean Chileans are very fond of seafood. *Erizos*, giant sea urchins, are a great delicacy. These are eaten raw with onion, lime juice, salt and pepper.
- Chile is South America's largest producer of minerals (except for oil). Over three-quarters of the country's export earnings come from copper.
- On Easter Day 1722 a Dutch expedition discovered an island 3,700 km west of Chile in the Pacific Ocean, which they called Easter Island. When they went ashore they found the island contained huge stone statues carved from volcanic rock and wooden tablets bearing a form of writing, the origin of which is still a mystery. Today Easter Island belongs to Chile and is a popular destination for tourists.
- Chilean fishermen catch 220 species of edible fish and shellfish.

China

Official name: People's Republic of China
History: China became a Communist republic in 1949. In the summer of 1989 students in Beijing led demonstrations for greater freedom. These were crushed by the army and thousands of people were reported to have been killed.
World location: Asia. China is the third largest country in the world and occupies most of the centre of Asia.
Area: 9,561,000 km^2
Local time: 8 hours ahead of GMT (summer time 9 hours ahead)
Population: 1,104,000,000
Language: Chinese. Several different dialects are spoken, the main one being based on the language of north China, sometimes called Mandarin.
Religion: Confucianism and Buddhism are the main religions in China. There are smaller numbers of Taoists and Moslems.
Capital: Beijing (Peking)
Other major centres: Shanghai, Tianjin, Shenyang, Wuhan, Guangzhou (Canton), Chongqing, Harbin, Chengdu, Xian, Zibo
Money: Yuan = 100 fen
Weather: Great variation: long, cold winters in the north, sub-tropical in the far south, dry in the northwestern deserts, monsoons in the east
Main rivers: Changjiang (Yangtze Kiang), Huanghe (Yellow River), Mekong
Main mountain ranges: Himalayas, Kunlun Shan, Tien Shan, Nan Shan
National day: 1 October
National flag: Red with one large and four smaller gold stars in the upper corner nearest the flagpole.

- The Chinese name for China means 'The Middle Kingdom'.
- Almost a fifth of the earth's inhabitants live in China.
- The commonest surname in the world is Chang. It is estimated that there are 104,000,000 people with this name.
- The Imperial Palace in Beijing is the world's largest palace. It is also surrounded by the world's largest moat.
- About 94 per cent of the Chinese people belong to the Han nationality, which has been the largest nationality in China for centuries.
- There are estimated to be 210,000,000 bicycles in China.
- The Chinese invented fireworks and the wheelbarrow.
- The secret of spinning silk from the thread of the silkworm cocoon originated in China. For centuries the Chinese kept the secret to themselves, but some time in the second or third centuries BC the secret of how to make silk was taken to Central Asia, from where it spread to Europe.
- The largest tomb yet discovered is that of the first Emperor of China who was buried at Mount Li. Found buried with him was the so-called Terracotta Army of 8,000 life-size clay soldiers.
- The first emperor of China began building the Great Wall of China to keep out invaders from the north. When it was completed by his successors, the wall was 6,400 km long; It is the first man-made object seen by the crews of space craft as they return to earth.
- China has more international frontiers than any other country and borders on thirteen other countries: Hong Kong, Macau, Vietnam, Laos, Burma, Bhutan, Nepal, India, Pakistan, Afghanistan, Mongolia, USSR, North Korea.
- China is the world's leading producer of cotton, tobacco and coal.
- Wall posters are a common means of communicating in

China. Large posters are put up on walls in public places and people use them to write down their opinions on subjects in the news.

- The principal food for the people of southern China is rice; in the north of the country the people prefer wheat, which they make into bread and noodles. It is said that a pasta resembling spaghetti was originally brought back to Italy by travellers who went to China in the Middle Ages. Meat makes up only a small part of the Chinese diet and many families only eat meat on special occasions. Soya beans, eggs, fish and poultry take its place for millions of people. China tea, the national drink, has become famous the world over.

- All over China you can see groups of people performing what looks like a dance in slow motion. They are actually practising a traditional Chinese exercise known as *tai chi chuan*, which consists of a series of exercises based on correct relaxation, balance and breathing.

- Among many developments China has brought to the west is the growing use of acupuncture. This is a traditional form of medicine in China that uses thin needles carefully placed in certain parts of the body to relieve pain or treat disease.

Christmas Island

History: Christmas Island was part of the Colony of Singapore until 1958 when Australia took control.
World location: Eastern Indian Ocean, 1,410 km north-west of Australia
Area: 135 km^2
Local time: 7 hours ahead of GMT
Population: 2,000
Language: English

Religion: Christian
Capital: Flying Fish Cove
Money: Australian dollar = 100 cents
Weather: Sub-tropical, warm all year.

- Christmas Island was sighted by Captain William Mynors's expedition on Christmas Day 1615, which is how it got its name.
- The island's most important export has been guano, bird droppings that have turned into phosphates over centuries. These are used for fertilisers.

Colombia

Official name: Republic of Colombia
History: A Spanish colony from the 16th century, Colombia gained independence in 1819.
World location: North-west of South America, with coastlines on the Pacific Ocean and the Atlantic Ocean
Area: 1,138,914 km^2
Local time: 5 hours behind GMT
Population: 30,240,000
Language: Spanish
Religion: Christian (Roman Catholic)
Capital: Bogota
Other major centres: Medellin, Cali, Barranquilla, Cartagena, Cucuta
Money: Colombian peso = 100 centavos
Weather: The coastal areas and lowland jungles are hot and humid. The Andean highlands are cooler and fresher.
Main rivers: Magdalena, Cauca, Amazon
Main mountain range: Andes
National day: 20 July

Colombia

National flag: Horizontal yellow stripe in the upper half with horizontal stripes of dark blue and red in the lower half.

- Tutenedo in Colombia is the wettest place on earth. Every year an average of 11,770 mm of rain falls there.
- Colombia is the only South American country to have coastlines on both the Atlantic and Pacific Oceans.
- Almost three-fifths of Colombia is uninhabited tropical lowland.
- Even in 1978 only just over a quarter of the Colombian children who began primary education stayed at school until they had completed this first stage.
- Colombia is the home of the marine toad, the largest toad in the world. Females can lay 35,000 eggs in a year. The Golden poison dart frog, the world's most poisonous, also lives in Colombia. There is enough poison in the average adult to kill 1,500 people.
- In general Colombians eat stews and thick soups, one favourite soup being *ajiaco*, made from potatoes, chicken and corn. Both adults and children enjoy *agua de panela*, a drink of brown sugar dissolved in water.

Comoros

Official name: Federal Islamic Republic of Comoros
History: The three islands came under French protection at the end of the 19th century. They became independent in 1975.
World location: Western Indian Ocean. The Comoros lie off the east African coast of Mozambique.
Area: 1,862 km^2
Local time: 3 hours ahead of GMT
Population: 490,000

Language: Comoran
Religion: Moslem
Capital: Moroni
Money: CFA franc = 100 centimes
Weather: Tropical, with two seasons: hot and humid from November to April and dry from May to October
National day: 6 July
National flag: Red horizontal stripe about twice the width of the green horizontal stripe below it. In the upper corner of the red area nearest the flagpole is a white crescent and four white stars.

- The Coelacanth, a prehistoric fish, thought to have been extinct for millions of years, gave scientists a surprise in the 1950s when one was caught alive off the coast of the Comoros.
- The Comoros provide two very important ingredients used in cooking in many parts of the world – cloves and vanilla. These are two of the islands' main exports, along with copra, maize and fragrant oils like citronella, ylang-ylang and lemon grass.

Congo

Official name: People's Republic of the Congo
History: The Congo was another of the four territories that made up French Equatorial Africa. It gained full independence in 1960.
World location: West central Africa
Area: 342,000 km^2
Local time: 1 hour ahead of GMT
Population: 1,890,000
Language: French is the official language, but local languages are commonly spoken as well.

Congo

Religion: Three-quarters of the population are Christians and there are smaller groups who follow traditional local religions and Islam.
Capital: Brazzaville
Other major centres: Pointe-Noire, N'Kayi, Loubomo
Money: CFA franc = 100 centimes
Weather: Hot and humid with tropical rains for seven or eight months a year
Main rivers: Zaire (Congo), Oubangui
National day: 15 August
National flag: Red, with a yellow hammer and hoe above which is a yellow star all surrounded by green wreaths.

- The Congo has one of the longest transportation systems in Africa, the Congo-Ocean railroad which is 515 km long.
- The Zaire River is the second largest river in Africa and with its tributaries it drains an area that is second in the world to that drained by the Amazon. Together with its tributaries the Zaire provides 12,000 km of navigable waterways.
- The dense tropical rainforests of the Congo are home of a very rare animal called the okapi, which was only scientifically identified at the beginning of this century. The okapi is a relative of the giraffe, although it is much smaller, standing about the size of a mule. It is well coloured for living in the jungle, having a dark brown body, with white stripes on its legs, which help it blend into the shadows cast in the thick foliage. In spite of having been discovered comparatively recently, the okapi is thought to have been in existence for thirty million years.

Cook Islands

History: The Cook Islands came under British protection in the 19th century and were transferred to New Zealand in 1901.
World location: South central Pacific Ocean. Two main groups of islands spread over a large area 3,000 km north-east of New Zealand.
Area: 293 km²
Local time: 9½ hours behind GMT (October to March 10 hours behind)
Population: 20,000
Language: English; Maori is also spoken
Religion: Christian
Capital: Avarua
Money: Cook Island dollar = 100 cents
Weather: Warm and humid

- Today many Cook Islanders work on their own plantations instead of those belonging to other people, which used to be the case in the past. They grow bananas, pineapples and citrus fruits. These form the islands' main exports, along with copra, clothing and pearl shell.

Costa Rica

Official name: Republic of Costa Rica
History: A Spanish colony from the 16th century, Costa Rica became independent in 1821
World location: Central America. The Caribbean Sea lies to the east, the Pacific Ocean to the west.
Area: 51,100 km²
Local time: Six hours behind GMT

Costa Rica

Population: 2,850,000
Language: Spanish
Religion: Christian (Roman Catholic)
Capital: San Jose
Other major centres: Limon, Alajuela, Puntarenas
Money: Costa Rican colon = 100 centimos
Weather: Hot in both coastal areas. The central plateau is cooler. The Caribbean coast is wetter than the Pacific coast.
Main river: Rio Grande
Main mountain ranges: Cordillera del Guanacaste, Cordillera de Tamanca
National day: 15 September
National flag: Five horizontal bands of blue, white, red, white, blue. The red band is twice the width of the others. The national coat of arms appears on a white disc near the flagpole.

- The name Costa Rica means 'Rich Coast' in Spanish. This was the name that Christopher Columbus gave the country possibly because of the ornaments made from gold that he saw the native Indians wearing.
- Three quarters of Costa Rica is covered by forests. Among the trees that grow there is the balsa tree which produces the lightest wood in the world. Each cubic metre of balsa wood weighs just 40 kg. Balsa wood is used to make model aircraft.
- In 1948 the army was abolished in Costa Rica. The country has never had compulsory military service and the army was replaced by the Civil Guard. The Civil Guard also operates an airborne section that has fifteen light aeroplanes and helicopters.
- Costa Rica has a very high level of people who can read and write. Elementary schooling is compulsory and both primary and secondary education is available to everyone in the country for no charge.
- The diet of most Costa Ricans is made up of beans,

corn, eggs and rice. Tropical fruits like bananas, mangos and pineapple are eaten too, and on special occasions there are exotic dishes like boiled iguana eggs and cooked hog's head.

Côte d'Ivoire

Official name: Republic of Côte d'Ivoire
History: A French colony from the end of the 19th century, the Côte d'Ivoire became independent in 1960.
World location: West Africa, with its southern coastline on the Atlantic Ocean
Area: 322,463 km^2
Local time: GMT
Population: 11,610,000
Language: French is the official language; local languages are spoken as well.
Religion: The largest religious group practise traditional local religions. The next largest are Christians, followed by the Moslem community.
Capital: Abidjan
Other major centres: Bouaké, Daloa, Man
Money: CFA franc = 100 centimes
Weather: Hot, wet and humid
Main rivers: Bandama, Sassandra, Komoé
Main mountain ranges: Man Mountains, Guinea Highlands
National day: 7 December
National flag: Three vertical stripes of orange, white and green.

● The Côte d'Ivoire is one of the most important wood-carving centres in Africa. Carved furniture, doors and wooden masks are made here.

- Masks are not only used for decoration in Côte d'Ivoire. One called 'Mother of Masks' is used to help patch up quarrels.
- About one worker in five in the Côte d'Ivoire comes from a neighbouring country.

Cuba

Official name: Republic of Cuba

History: Cuba was a Spanish possession for most of its history from the sixteenth century until it became independent in 1898. The country became a Communist republic in 1959.

World location: West Indies, at the entrance to the Gulf of Mexico

Area: 110,860 km^2

Local time: 5 hours behind GMT

Population: 10,400,000

Language: Spanish

Religion: There is no state religion in Cuba. Christianity (Roman Catholicism) is the main religion among the people.

Capital: Havana

Other major centres: Santiago de Cuba, Camaguey, Holguin

Money: Cuban peso = 100 centavos

Weather: Sub-tropical with rains from May to October

Main river: Cauto

Main mountain range: Sierra Maestra

National day: 1 January

National flag: Five horizontal stripes of blue, white, blue, white, blue. Near the flagpole is a red triangle bearing a white star.

- One of the largest specimens of the Great White Shark ever caught was hooked off the coast of Cuba. The Great White is the largest meat-eating shark and this particular one measured 6.4 metres in length.
- Cuba is also the home of the world's smallest bird, the tiny Bee Hummingbird.
- When Christopher Columbus discovered Cuba in 1492 he named it Cuba Juana, after one of the children of the King and Queen of Spain who were paying for his expedition. Cubanacan was the name given to the island by the Indians living there when Columbus arrived.
- Cuba is the world's second largest sugar producer, with sugar and its by-products earning half its income from foreign countries.

Cyprus

Official name: Republic of Cyprus
History: Cyprus has been controlled by many nations since ancient times. The Turks conquered the island in the 16th century and the British took possession of it in the 19th century. Cyprus became independent in 1960. In 1974 fighting between Greeks and Turks led to the island being split into a Turkish-controlled northern area and a Greek-controlled south.
World location: Eastern Mediterranean Sea
Area: 9,251 km^2
Local time: 2 hours ahead of GMT
Population: 690,000
Language: Greek and Turkish
Religion: Christian (Greek Orthodox); Moslem
Capital: Nicosia
Other major centres: Limassol, Larnaca, Paphos

Cuba

Money: Cyprus pound = 100 cents
Weather: Hot dry summers; colder winters with snow on the mountains
Main rivers: Seranhis, Pedieas
Main mountain ranges: Trodos, Kyrenian Mountains
National day: 1 October
National flag: White, with a yellow map of the island above two olive branches.

- Copper has been mined on Cyprus since ancient times and the island is named after the Greek word for 'copper', *kypros*. The only breed of wild sheep left in Europe lives on Cyprus. It is called the Cyprus Moufflon and is protected in special nature reserves.
- In ancient times Cyprus was famous for its forests but today these cover just one-fifth of the island.
- Both English and French are compulsory subjects in schools in Cyprus.
- The Greek and Turkish parts of Cyprus are so separated that there are no public transport systems linking the two.

Czechoslovakia

Official name: Czechoslovak Socialist Republic
History: Originally part of the Austro-Hungarian Empire, Czechoslovakia was made independent in 1919. Germany occupied the country during the Second World War and it became a Communist republic in 1948. Twenty years later, attempts to reform the Communist party were ended by an invasion from the USSR. However, in 1989 there were widespread popular demonstrations against the Communist leaders, which led to important changes in the government, bringing

much greater freedom and a non-Communist government.

World location: Central Europe
Area: 127,903 km²
Local time: 1 hour ahead of GMT
Population: 15,570,000
Language: Czech and Slovak
Religion: Christian; the Roman Catholic Church is the largest.
Capital: Prague
Other major centres: Bratislava, Brno, Ostrava, Košice, Plzeň
Money: Koruna = 100 haler
Weather: Warm, rainy summers; cold winters
Main rivers: Labe (Elbe), Vltava (Moldau), Dunaj (Danube)
Main mountain ranges: Bohemian-Moravian Highlands, Krkonose, Tatras
National day: 9 May
National flag: Two horizontal stripes of white and red with a blue triangle next to the flagpole. The red and white represent Bohemia and the blue Moravia, two of the provinces of the old Austro-Hungarian Empire from which Czechoslovakia was created.

- St Wenceslaus, the 'Good King Wenceslas' of the Christmas song, was a Bohemian duke who ruled part of Bohemia in the tenth century. He encouraged the growth of Christianity in Bohemia, but his mother did not agree with him. Probably at her suggestion Wenceslaus was killed by his brother Boleslaw in 935 when he was only thirty-two years old.
- The playwright William Shakespeare sets part of his play *The Winter's Tale* in Bohemia. However, he gives the country a coastline whereas the real Bohemia is landlocked and far from the sea.

Denmark

Official name: Kingdom of Denmark
History: Denmark as we know it today came into being in 1815, although it has been a unified country since the 10th century and at one time controlled Norway.
World location: Northern Europe
Area: 43,069 km^2
Local time: 1 hour ahead of GMT
Population: 5,130,000
Language: Danish
Religion: Christian (Evangelical Lutheran)
Capital: Copenhagen
Other major centres: Aarhus, Odense, Aalborg, Esbjerg
Money: Danish krone = 100 ore
Weather: Mild summers and cold winters
Main river: Gudenå
National day: 16 April
National flag: Red with a white cross. The Danish flag is called the Dannebrog, meaning the 'Strength of Denmark'. It is one of the oldest flags in use today and originated in 1219 from a vision seen by King Waldemar of Denmark just before a battle.

- The storywriter Hans Christian Andersen was born in the city of Odense.
- Lego was invented in Denmark and there is a theme park called Legoland to celebrate this. Among the exhibits is a statue of the Indian Chief Sitting Bull which stands 7.6 metres high and is made of 1,500,000 Lego bricks.
- Denmark is one of the most efficient farming countries in Europe and yet almost half the farms in the country have fewer than ten hectares of land.
- One person in four in Denmark lives in Copenhagen.

- King Canute, the King of England who showed that he could not make the sea turn back according to one popular story, was also King of Denmark and King of Norway. This large kingdom was divided after he died in 1035.
- The Tivoli Gardens in Copenhagen have a military band made up of boys aged from ten to sixteen. As well as playing the same sort of musical instruments that army bands play, they wear a uniform very like that worn by the Royal Guard.
- The world's most accurate clockwork clock has been installed in the Town Hall in Copenhagen. Called the Olsen Clock, this is so accurate that it will lose only half a second in 300 years.
- Most Danes eat four meals a day: breakfast, lunch, dinner and a late evening supper. In most homes the only hot meal is dinner. The Danes are famous for their *smørrebrød*, a selection of delicious toppings to put on open sandwiches. One sandwich may be a pyramid of twenty small shrimps on a thin slice of bread.

Djibouti

Official name: Republic of Djibouti
History: Formerly a French territory, Djibouti became independent in 1977.
World location: North-east Africa, on the Gulf of Aden
Area: 23,200 km^2
Local time: 3 hours ahead of GMT
Population: 380,000
Language: French is the official language; Somali, Afar and Arabic are also spoken.
Religion: Moslem
Capital: Djibouti

Djibouti

Other major centres: Tasjoura, Obock, Dikhil
Money: Djibouti franc = 100 centimes
Weather: Very hot and dry throughout the year
National day: 27 June
National flag: Two horizontal stripes of blue and green, with a white triangle next to the flagpole containing a red star.

- Almost 90 per cent of Djibouti is bare desert. Only one per cent of the land can be used for farming.
- Two out of every three people in Djibouti are nomads who live in the desert with their flocks, moving from camp to camp with no permanent home.
- As recently as 1983 almost 90 per cent of the roads in Djibouti had no hard surface.

Dominica

Official name: Commonwealth of Dominica
History: Dominica was a British colony until it became independent in 1978
World location: Eastern Caribbean Sea. Dominica is the most northerly of the Windward Islands.
Area: 751 km^2
Local time: 4 hours behind GMT
Population: 80,000
Language: English; local French dialect
Religion: Christian (mainly Roman Catholic)
Capital: Roseau
Money: East Caribbean dollar = 100 cents
Weather: Tropical with a rainy season from June to October
Main river: Layou
National day: 3 November

National flag: British blue ensign with the national coat of arms on the edge furthest from the flagpole.

- Christopher Columbus gave the islands their name to commemmorate the day he discovered them, Sunday (*Dies Dominica*) 3 November, 1493.
- When the Spanish arrived in the 15th century they found Dominica inhabited by the Caribs, a people who had migrated from the Amazon region of South America. They were a warlike race who fought fiercely against the new arrivals and remained almost the only people living on the island until the 18th century. The Caribs gave their name to the Caribbean Sea.
- Among its exports Dominica sends lime juice overseas to be used for making lime cordials, cosmetics and sweets.
- Dominica shows signs of volcanic activity in its mountains. In places there are hot springs and the so-called Boiling Lake in the south of the island gives off gasses that can sometimes be poisonous.

Dominican Republic

History: The Dominican Republic was a Spanish colony until its independence in 1821. From 1822 to 1844 it was occupied by neighbouring Haiti, and from 1916 until 1924 US marines occupied the country.
World location: Caribbean Sea. The Dominican Republic occupies the eastern part of the island of Hispaniola (the western part belongs to Haiti).
Area: 48,734 km^2
Local time: 4 hours behind GMT
Population: 6,870,000
Language: Spanish

Dominican Republic

Religion: Christian (Roman Catholic)
Capital: Santo Domingo
Other major centres: Santiago de los Caballeros, La Romana, San Pedro de Macoris
Money: Dominican Republic peso = 100 centavos
Weather: Sub-tropical; the mountains are cooler. The Dominican Republic lies in the path of hurricanes.
Main river: Yaque del Norte
Main mountain range: Cordillera Central
National day: 27 February
National flag: Red and blue with a white cross, at the centre of which is the national emblem.

- The Dominican Republic is the oldest European settlement anywhere in America. Christopher Columbus landed here in 1492.
- Nelson de la Rose, the world's shortest man, lives in the Dominican Republic. He stands 72 cm high.
- Between 1563 and 1736 the bones of Christopher Columbus and his son Diego were buried in the cathedral in Santo Domingo, from where they were transferred first to Havana, and then in 1902 back to Seville in Spain.

Ecuador

Official name: Republic of Ecuador
History: Ecuador was first conquered by the Incas from Peru and in the 16th century conquered by Spain. The country remained a Spanish colony until 1822 when it won its independence.
World location: North-west of South America, with its western coastline on the Pacific Ocean
Area: 283,561 km²

Local time: 5 hours behind GMT (Galapagos Islands 6 hours behind GMT)
Population: 10,200,000
Language: Spanish; local Indian languages like Quecha are also spoken.
Religion: Christian (Roman Catholic)
Capital: Quito
Other major centres: Guayaquil, Cuenca, Portoviejo
Money: Sucre = 100 centavos
Weather: Hot and humid by the coast, milder with cool nights in the higher regions
Main rivers: Napo, Pastaza, Curaray
Main mountain range: Andes
National day: 10 August
National flag: Three horizontal stripes of yellow, blue and red. The yellow stripe is twice the width of the others. In the centre is the national coat of arms above which is a large bird of prey called a condor.

- Ecuador is the second smallest republic in South America.
- The country is named after the Equator that runs through its northern area and is marked by a monument carrying a globe.
- Except for farmland on the coast and in the river valleys, and pastureland in the Andean highlands, Ecuador is one huge forest covering a total area of 233,100 km^2 – over five and a half times the size of Switzerland.
- Growing bananas is very important in Ecuador and the country exports more bananas than any other in the world.
- Potatoes form an important part of the diet in Ecuador as they do in neighbouring countries in the Andes mountains of South America. *Locro*, a thick soup made from cheese and potatoes, is a popular dish. So are *llapingachos*, fried potato and cheese cakes, served with a peanut sauce.

Egypt

Official name: Arab Republic of Egypt

History: Egypt's history has been recorded since ancient times. From the 16th century until the outbreak of the First World War in 1914 Egypt was part of the Ottoman Empire centred on present-day Turkey. It then came under British protection until 1922 when an independent kingdom was created. Egypt became a republic in 1953.

World location: North-east Africa. Egypt forms the north-east corner of the continent with shores on the Mediterranean Sea to the north and the Red Sea to the east.

Area: 1,001,449 km²

Local Time: 2 hours ahead of GMT

Population: 51,900,000

Language: Arabic

Religion: Moslem; small Christian community

Capital: Cairo

Other major centres: Alexandria, Gaza, Shubra-alKhayma, Port Said

Money: Egyptian pound = 100 piastres

Weather: Dry and hot; more than nine-tenths of the country is desert.

Main river: Nile

Main mountain ranges: Sinai, Eastern Coastal Range

National day: 23 July

National flag: Three horizontal stripes of red, white and black with the national emblem of a yellow eagle above a scroll on which is written in Arabic 'Arab Republic of Egypt'.

- The three Pyramids of Gaza are the only 'wonder' of the seven wonders of the Ancient World still standing.
- The River Nile is the longest river in Africa and experts

differ as to whether the Nile or the Amazon is the longest river in the world.

- Only about one twenty-eighth of the land in Egypt can be settled and used for farming. The rest is desert.
- Cleopatra, who was one of the most famous rulers of ancient Egypt, wasn't Egyptian at all. She was Greek.
- The ancient Egyptians used to preserve the bodies of important people as mummies. The oldest surviving mummy is that of a court musician called Wati. His mummy dates back to about 2,400 BC
- The ancient Egyptians used a system of picture writing known as hieroglyphics. Until the early nineteenth century no one had been able to translate this. Then a group of French scholars who were in Egypt during Napoleon's occupation of the country discovered an important key in solving the mystery. This was the Rosetta Stone, a large stone slab on which was written an inscription in hieroglyphics with a translation in Greek. The scholars were able to translate the Greek easily and by doing this they were able to piece together what the hieroglyphics meant, and so discover the meaning of all the ancient inscriptions in Egypt.
- Children in ancient Egypt may have played marbles using nuts or pebbles instead of the glass marbles we use today.

El Salvador

Official name: Republic of El Salvador
History: El Salvador was a Spanish colony from the 16th century until 1821.
World location: Central America, with its western coastline on the Pacific Ocean
Area: 21,393 km²

El Salvador

Local time: 6 hours behind GMT
Population: 5,110,000
Language: Spanish
Religion: Christian (Roman Catholic)
Capital: San Salvador
Other major centres: Santa Ana, San Miguel, Nueva San Salvador
Money: El Salvador colon = 100 centavos
Weather: Hot and humid in the coastal areas, cooler in the mountains
Main rivers: Lempa, San Miguel
National day: 15 September
National flag: Three horizontal stripes of blue, white, blue with the country's coat of arms in the middle of the blue stripe.

- The capital, San Salvador, was named after the Roman Catholic feast of San Salvador del Mundo, which means 'Holy Saviour of the World'.
- Half the money El Salvador earns from other countries comes from selling coffee.
- El Salvador is the world's largest supplier of a medicinal gum called balsam.
- Most Salvadorians eat beans, bread, corn and rice. A special snack called *papusas* is very popular. This is a cake stuffed with chopped meat, beans and spices.

Equatorial Guinea

Official name: Republic of Equatorial Guinea
History: A Spanish colony, Equatorial Guinea became independent in 1968
World location: West central Africa, with its western coastline on the Atlantic Ocean (Gulf of Guinea)

Area: 28,051 km^2
Local time: 1 hour ahead of GMT
Population: 420,000
Language: Spanish is the official language.
Religion: Christian (Roman Catholic)
Capital: Malabo
Other major centre: Mikomeseng
Money: CFA franc = 100 centimes
Weather: Hot and humid with heavy rainfall
Main rivers: Campo, Benito, Muni
National day: 12 October
National flag: Three horizontal stripes of green, white and red, with a blue triangle next to the flagpole. The national coat of arms is in the centre of the white stripe.

- Unlike Portugal in the great days of its empire, the Spanish empire had very few colonies in Africa and Equatorial Guinea was the only Spanish colony south of the Sahara desert.
- Equatorial Guinea is the home of the world's first recorded albino gorilla. His name is Snowflake and he has blue eyes.

Ethiopia

Official name: Socialist Ethiopia
History: Ethiopia was once a powerful empire in east Africa. Italy occupied the country from 1936 until 1941. The last emperor was deposed in 1974 and the country became a socialist republic. Ethiopia suffered very serious famines in 1984 and 1989 which were made worse in parts of the country by civil war.
World location: North-east Africa, with its north-eastern coastline on the Red Sea

Ethiopia

Area: 1,221,900 km^2
Local time: 3 hours ahead of GMT
Population: 47,880,000
Language: Amharic, Somali, Arabic
Religion: Moslem and Christian (mainly Ethiopian Orthodox)
Capital: Addis Abbaba
Other major centres: Dire Dawa, Nazret, Bahr Dar
Money: Birr = 100 cents
Weather: Hot and very dry in desert areas, cooler on the high plateaux. In several recent years there has been very little rain in Ethiopia, leading to the shortage of food and widespread starvation mentioned above.
Main rivers: Abbay, Tekeze, Awash
Main mountain ranges: Eritrean Highlands, Tigre Plateau, Eastern Highlands
National day: 12 September
National flag: Three horizontal stripes of green, yellow and red.

- According to legend the Queen of Sheba, who is mentioned in the Old Testament, once lived in what we call Ethiopia. Her son Menelik traditionally founded the Ethiopian royal line at about 1000 BC.
- Archaeologists have found evidence of the world's earliest known industry in Ethiopia. This was the craft of flint knapping – the chopping and shaping of tools and axes made from flint. In Ethiopia flint knapping was taking place 2,500,000 years ago.
- Ethiopia has fewer doctors per head of population than any other country. In 1977 there was only one doctor for every 75,000 people.
- In 1974 ninety-five people out of every hundred in Ethiopia were unable to read or write. Since then the government claims to have improved the figures. Government figures state that almost half the population can now read and write.

- A lot of food in Ethiopia is eaten with a pancake-like bread called *injera*, which is used in place of knives and forks to lift the food from plates for eating.

Faroe Islands

History: From the 14th century until the 18th century the Faroe Islands belonged to Norway. Since 1948 they have been a self-governing region of Denmark.
World location: North Atlantic Ocean
Area: 1,399 km²
Local time: GMT
Population: 50,000
Language: Faroese and Danish
Religion: Christian (mainly Lutheran)
Capital: Torshavn
Money: Faroese krona = 100 ore
Weather: Cool
National flag: Although the islands belong to Denmark they have their own flag which is white with a red cross, edged with blue.

- In Danish the Faroe Islands mean the 'Sheep Islands', and the islanders have been famous for their wool and woollen garments for centuries.
- Only 2 per cent of the land in the Faroes is cultivated. The rest is given over to grazing.

Falkland Islands

Official name: Colony of the Falkland Islands and Dependencies

History: There has been a British colony on the Falkland Islands continually since 1832. Argentina claims the islands and occupied them from April to June 1982.

World location: South Atlantic, off the east coast of South America

Area: 12,173 km²

Local time: 3 hours behind GMT (summer time 4 hours behind)

Population: 1,900

Language: English

Religion: Christian (Church of England)

Capital: Port Stanley

Money: Falkland Islands pound = 100 pence

Weather: Cool, with strong winds

National flag: The Falkland Islands flag is a British Blue Ensign with the badge of the island.

- Most of the land in the Falklands is used for sheep grazing and there are roughly 370 sheep for every Falkland islander.
- Three-quarters of the children in the Falkland Islands go to school in Port Stanley. The others are taught in small schools in settlements around the islands, or receive lessons from teachers who travel to their homes.

Fiji

Official name: Republic of Fiji
History: Fiji became a British colony in 1874 and gained independence in 1970.
World location: South central Pacific Ocean
Area: 18,333 km^2
Local time: 12 hours ahead of GMT
Population: 730,000
Language: English, Fijian, Hindi
Religion: Christian and Hindu, with a small community of Moslems
Capital: Suva
Other major centre: Lautoka
Money: Fiji dollar = 100 cents
Weather: Tropical with ocean breezes that prevent it becoming too hot or humid
Main rivers: Rewa, Sigatoka, Navua
National day: 10 October
National flag: Light blue, with the Union Jack in the upper corner next to the flagpole and the country's coat of arms.

- Fijians have the lowest rate of colour blindness in the world.
- In 1979 a new species of reptile was discovered in Fiji and was given the name of Fijian crested iguana.
- The first detailed description of Fiji was written by a famous British sailor named Captain William Bligh. He was the commander of the *Bounty* when the sailors mutinied against him during a voyage from Tahiti in 1789. Bligh and eighteen men were cast adrift in a small boat with only a few provisions and no chart. Forty-seven days later they sighted land — what is today Papua New Guinea — after suffering terrible hardships and having sailed their little boat 9,370 km across the ocean.

- The Fijian diet reflects the country's history. The Fijian love of seafood such as baby octopus, shark and turtles shows the islanders' historic association with the sea. However, they also eat a great deal of corned beef, which has been imported into Fiji for 200 years after the first Europeans to land in Fiji shared some of their ship's rations with the islanders.

Finland

Official name: Republic of Finland
History: From the Middle Ages until the 18th century Finland belonged to Sweden. It then became part of Russia until 1917, when Finland declared itself independent during the Russian Revolution.
World location: Northern Europe, with its coastline on the Baltic Sea
Area: 338,145 km^2
Local time: Two hours ahead of GMT
Population: 4,950,000
Language: Finnish and Swedish
Religion: Christian (Lutheran and Greek Orthodox)
Capital: Helsinki
Other major centres: Tampere, Turku, Espoo
Money: Marka = 100 penni
Weather: Warm summers, very long cold winters
Main rivers: Paatsjoki, Torniojoki, Kemijoki
Main mountain ranges: Suomenselkä, Maanselkä
National day: 6 December
National flag: White with a blue cross. The blue and white represent the many lakes and snowfields of Finland.

- The most famous feature of Finnish life is a special kind of of bath called a *sauna*. People take a sauna to relax in the very hot temperatures that can reach as high as 100°C.

- Winter sports such as ice hockey, skating and ski-jumping are popular in Finland, but the Finns also have a summer game which is unique to their homeland. This is a form of baseball called *pesapallo*, which means 'nest-ball' in English. The game was created early this century and was fully developed by 1922. The bat and ball are lighter than those used in baseball and the batsmen have to run a zig-zag course between bases which are placed increasingly further apart.
- Finland is the most densely forested country in Europe, with two-thirds of the land covered by trees.
- The Finns make excellent sausages. Those made from reindeer meat are called *poromakkara*. Others are known as *saunamakkara*, named after the Finnish sauna because the sausages are usually cooked on the sauna stove. The sauna is also an ideal place to hang hams and mutton to be smoked.

France

Official name: French Republic
History: France was ruled by kings until the French Revolution. The first republic was established in 1792. Germany occupied France during the Second World War.
World location: Western Europe, with its northern coastline on the English Channel, its western on the Atlantic Ocean and its southern on the Mediterranean Sea
Area: 534,965 km²
Local time: 1 hour ahead of GMT (summer time 2 hours ahead)

France

Population: 55,870,000
Language: French
Religion: Christian (mainly Roman Catholic)
Capital: Paris
Other major centres: Lyon, Marseille, Lille, Bordeaux, Toulouse, Nantes, Nice, Toulon, Grenoble
Money: Franc = 100 centimes
Weather: The south has warm summers and mild winters. The north is cooler and there are heavy snowfalls in the eastern and southern mountains in winter.
Main rivers: Rhône, Seine, Loire, Garonne
Main mountain ranges: Alps, Massif Central, Pyrenees, Jura, Vosges
National day: 14 July
National flag: The 'tricolour' with three vertical stripes of blue, white and red. Due to a strange optical illusion the red stripe would appear to be narrower than the other two if they were all the same width. To make them look the same width the blue stripe occupies 33 per cent of the flag, the white stripe 30 per cent and the red stripe 37 per cent.

- France is the largest country in Western Europe. Among other European nations it is second only to the USSR in area.
- The Louvre, in Paris, is one of the largest art museums in the world. Its collection has nearly 250,000 drawings, paintings, statues and other works of art. These include the *Mona Lisa* painted by Leonardo da Vinci, which once hung in Napoleon's bathroom. Over 2,000,000 visitors go to the Louvre every year.
- The greatest national sporting event in France each year is the Tour de France, a cycle race in which over 100 cyclists from all over the world pedal round France as fast as they can for a month, ending with a grand finish in Paris.

- Both the hot air balloon and the parachute were invented in France. The Montgolfier brothers invented the balloon and flew the first one in 1783. Two years later Jean-Pierre Blanchard invented the first parachute.
- 265 different kinds of cheese are made in France.
- The French railway system has developed some of the fastest trains in the world. These special high-speed trains called TGVs, can travel from Paris to Lyons in exactly two hours. The distance is 425 km and the trains average 212.5 km/hr. If the same train was running in the UK it would be possible to travel from London to Glasgow in a fraction over three hours.
- French cooking is probably the most celebrated in the world. Many regions of France have become famous for their particular specialities. The Guyenne region is well known for its truffles (mushroom-like plants that give certain foods a unique flavour); in Burgundy snails are very popular; and the Paris region is celebrated for its pressed duck. The wines of France are world famous too and these also have strong local connections: only the wines made in the area of Champagne can call themselves champagne and the vineyards in Bordeaux where some of the world's most famous wines are made contain some of the most expensive farming land in the world.
- There is a village in France called Y.

French Guiana

Official name: Department of French Guiana
History: French colony since the 17th century
World location: North-east of South America, with its coastline on the Atlantic Ocean
Area: 91,000 km²

French Guiana

Local time: 3 hours behind GMT
Population: 90,000
Language: French; Creole is also spoken.
Religion: Christian (mainly Roman Catholic)
Capital: Cayenne
Other major centres: Kourou, Saint-Laurent-de-Maroni
Money: Franc = 100 cents
Weather: Hot and humid with high rainfall
Main mountain range: Tumac-Humac Mountains

- Almost ninety per cent of French Guiana is covered with forests.
- A dish called Pepperpot is very popular in French Guiana. It is a meat stew to which is added a bitter vegetable juice called *cassareep*. Nobody could describe Pepperpot as fast food! Cooking takes several days as more meat and more *cassareep* are slowly added until the cook finally has enough to feed everyone.

French Polynesia

Official name: Territory of French Polynesia
History: The islands came under French protection in 1843
World location: South Central Pacific Ocean. There are about 130 islands spread over a large area.
Area: 4,200 km² (land area)
Local time: 9–10 hours ahead of GMT
Population: 170,000
Language: French; Polynesian languages are also spoken.
Religion: Christian
Capital: Papeete

Money: CFP franc = 100 centimes
Weather: Sub-tropical; sea breezes prevent it becoming too hot or too humid.

- For a month each year the Tiurai Festival takes place in which there are competitions for dancing, singing and canoe racing.
- Fish is the main ingredient of Polynesian food. *Poisson cru* (raw fish soaked in coconut milk and lime juice) is popular; so is *farfaru*, which has the unappetising English translation of 'smelly fish'.

Gabon

Official name: Gabonese Republic
History: A French colony from the 19th century, Gabon became independent in 1960.
World location: West central Africa with its western coastline on the Atlantic Ocean
Area: 267,667 km^2
Local time: 1 hour ahead of GMT
Population: 1,090,000
Language: French; Bantu languages are also spoken.
Religion: Christian; small following of traditional local religions
Capital: Libreville
Other major centres: Port-Gentil, Masuku
Money: CFA franc = 100 centimes
Weather: Hot and humid with heavy rainfall
Main river: Ogooué
National day: 17 August
National flag: Three horizontal stripes of green, yellow and blue.

Gabon

- Dr Albert Schweitzer, the famous German missionary doctor, gave up fame in Europe as a young man to devote his life to helping the sick in Africa, particularly sufferers from leprosy. In 1913 he built his hospital in Lambarene, then a deserted mission station in French West Africa. As well as the hospital he built a church where the Mass is still translated into two African dialects during the service.
- Almost 80 per cent of Gabon is covered by forest, an area almost equivalent to Scotland and England combined.

The Gambia

Official name: Republic of Gambia
History: Gambia was a British colony from the 19th century until it became independent in 1965
World location: West Africa, with a short western coastline on the Atlantic Ocean
Area: 11,295 km²
Local time: GMT
Population: 810,000
Language: English; local languages are also spoken
Religion: Mainly Moslem with a small number of Christians
Capital: Banjul
Other major centres: Serekunda, Bakau, Birkama
Money: Dalasi = 100 bututs
Weather: Two seasons: dry from November to May, wet from June to October. Hotter in the interior than on the coast
Main river: Gambia
National day: 18 February
National flag: Three large horizontal stripes of red, blue

and green, with narrow white stripes above and below
the central blue stripe.

- On land the Gambia is surrounded entirely by Senegal.
- Fishing is important in the Gambia and just 11 per cent
  of the fish caught come from inland waters.
- Gambians play a musical instrument called a *kora*, a
  type of many stringed guitar that dates back at least
  three centuries.

Germany

Official name : Federal Republic of Germany
History: Between the end of the Second World War in
1945 and 1990 Germany was divided into the Federal
Republic of Germany (also known as West Germany)
and the German Democratic Republic (East Germany).
The FDR was created out of the areas of Germany
occupied by France, the USA and the UK at the end of
the war. The GDR was formed from the part of Germany
occupied by the USSR. After the war, control of the city
of Berlin was divided between the USA, France and the
UK, who occupied the western part of the city, and the
USSR which occupied the eastern part. In 1961 the East
German authorities built a wall to divide the two parts of
the city. In 1989 people all over East Germany began
demonstrating for greater freedom in their country and
easier travel abroad. These demonstrations led to the fall
of the Communist government and the pulling down of
the Berlin wall. In October 1990 Germany was reunited.
World location: Northern Central Europe – Northern
coastlines on both the North Sea and the Baltic Sea.
Area: 357,039 km²

Germany

Local time: 1 hour ahead of GMT (summer time 2 hours ahead)
Population: 77,870,000
Language: German
Religion: Christian
Capital: Berlin (Bonn, the former capital of West Germany, is still the seat of government).
Other major centres: Hamburg, Munich, Cologne, Essen, Frankfurt-am-Main, Leipzig, Dresden.
Money: Deutsche Mark = 100 pfennig
Weather: Mild near the coasts. Inland the summers are hotter and the winters colder.
Main rivers: Rhein (Rhine), Ems, Weser, Elbe, Donau (Danube)
Main mountain ranges: Alps, Schwarzwald (Black Forest), Harz.
National day: 3 October
National flag: Three horizontal stripes of black, red and gold.

- The world's first mechanically printed book was a copy of the Bible printed in Mainz by Johann Gutenberg in about 1456.
- The world's oldest newspaper also came from Germany. This is a news pamphlet that was printed in Cologne in 1470.
- The Protestant cathedral in Ulm has the world's tallest cathedral spire with a height of 160.9 metres.
- The Piccolo Theatre in Hamburg has only thirty seats, making it the world's smallest theatre.
- In 1907 building work started on the world's first zoo without bars at Stellingen, near Hamburg. Instead of the cages in which zoo animals had been kept until then, animals in this new zoo were housed in big pits and large pens where they could roam freely without endangering visitors.
- Near Bergheim there is a huge hole in the ground which

has an area of 21 km² and is 324 metres deep. This is a manmade hole which has been dug since 1955. It's an opencast coal mine, where the coal deposits lie close enough to the surface to be dug out from above once the soil covering them has been cleared away.

- The Kiel Canal which runs through northern Germany to join the North Sea with the Baltic Sea carries more ships than any other big-ship canal in the world. Over twice as many ships pass through the Kiel Canal as through the Suez Canal.

- The world's first motor car manufacturing company started building cars in Mannheim in 1888. The company was created by Karl Benz who had built his first practical motor car three years earlier. Other designers in other countries were building cars before Benz, but his car was the first to be put into commercial production.

- X-rays used by doctors to examine inside their patients were first discovered and used by a scientist in Wurzburg. His name was Wilhelm Konrad Röntgen who made his historic discovery in November 1895. The first X-ray photograph he took was of his wife's hand and it clearly shows the bones beneath her skin as well as the wedding-ring on her ring finger.

- The Berlin Wall was over forty kilometres long, making it one of the longest walls in the world.

- In 1939 Berlin was the second largest city in continental Europe.

Ghana

Official name: Republic of Ghana
History: Ghana was a British colony until it became independent in 1957.
World location: West Africa, with its southern coastline on the Atlantic Ocean
Area: 238,537 km^2
Local Time: GMT
Population: 14,130,000
Language: English, Ashanti, Fanti
Religion: Christian; small Moslem community
Capital: Accra
Other major centres: Kumasi, Tamale, Tema
Money: Cedi = 100 pesawas
Weather: The north is hot and dry, further south there is greater rainfall and the humidity is higher.
Main rivers: Volta and its tributaries
National day: 6 March
National flag: Three horizontal stripes of red, yellow and green, with a black star in the middle of the yellow stripe.

- Ghana's Lake Volta is the largest artificial lake of its kind in the world. It has changed the lives of people living beside it to such an extent that many farmers have become fishermen instead.
- In the south of Ghana they wear a large, colourful cotton cloth called the *kente*. Traditionally this is made by the men.
- Ghana is only slightly smaller in area than the UK, yet its population is less than a quarter that of the UK.
- In Ghana drums are used to sound alarms and to send messages. Ghana is famous for its 'talking drums', which have an 'alphabet' of different tones. The pitch is

altered by tightening the drum skin for a higher tone, or
slackening it for a deeper one.

Gibraltar

Official name: Colony of Gibraltar
History: Gibraltar has been a British colony since the
18th century.
World location: South-west Europe. Gibraltar occupies
a narrow promontory on the southern coast of Spain at
the western entrance to the Mediterranean Sea.
Area: 6 km^2
Local time: 1 hour ahead of GMT (summer time 2
hours ahead)
Population: 30,000
Language: English and Spanish
Religion: Christian (mainly Roman Catholic)
Money: Gibraltar pound = 100 pence
Weather: Warm all through the year with rain falling
mainly in the winter
National flag: The flag of Gibraltar is the British Blue
Ensign with the colony's badge.

- St Michael's is one of the many caves in the rock of
  Gibraltar. This has attracted visitors since Roman times
  because of its amazing rock formations.
- Probably the best known residents of Gibraltar are the
  Rock apes, or Barbary apes. These are the only wild
  monkeys still living in Europe, and according to legend
  if they should ever disappear from the rock, British rule
  will end soon after.

Greece

Official name: Hellenic Republic

History: Greece has a recorded history, dating from ancient times. The country became independent from the Ottoman Empire (Turkey) in 1830. Germany occupied Greece during the Second World War. In 1967 the last king was deposed and the country declared a republic.

World location: South-eastern Europe. The mainland has coastlines on the Mediterranean Sea and the Aegean Sea. There are also many islands.

Area: 131,957 km^2

Local time: 2 hours ahead of GMT (summer time 3 hours ahead)

Population: 10,010,000

Language: Greek

Religion: Christian (Greek Orthodox)

Capital: Athens

Other major centres: Thessaloniki, Piraeus, Patras, Larissa

Money: Drachma = 100 lepta

Weather: Hot, dry summers and mild, wet winters. The north is colder than the south.

Main rivers: Aliakmon, Pinios, Akheloos

Main mountain ranges: Pindus Mountains

National day: 25 March

National flag: Nine horizontal stripes of blue and white, with a white cross on a blue background in the upper corner next to the flagpole.

- Greece is often said to be the birthplace of European civilization. The alphabets of most major European languages are based on the Greek one. The word alphabet comes from the first two Greek letters *alpha* and *beta*.

- One of the highlights of the feast of Saint Constantine celebrated in Greece every year is a fire-walking event.
- In the north of Greece is a peninsula called Mount Athos which has governed its own affairs for centuries. Mount Athos consists of twenty monasteries inhabited entirely by monks. No women and not even any female animals are allowed to set foot on the land the monks own.

Greenland

History: Greenland has belonged to Denmark since the 14th century. The island has been in charge of its internal affairs since 1981.
World location: Arctic Ocean
Area: 2,175,600 km²
Local time: 3–4 hours behind GMT
Population: 50,000
Language: Danish and Innuit (Eskimo)
Religion: Christian (Evangelical Lutheran)
Capital: Nuuk (Godthab)
Money: Danish Krone = 100 ore
Weather: Very cold

- Greenland is the largest island in the world. (In geographical terms Australia is a continent as opposed to an island.)
- Since the sea freezes over for most of the year the most practical way to travel on Greenland is by skidoo or dog sled pulled by teams of huskies.

Grenada

Official name: State of Grenada
History: A British colony from the 18th century, Grenada became independent in 1974.
World location: Eastern Caribbean Sea. Grenada is the most southerly of the Windward Islands.
Area: 334 km²
Local time: 4 hours behind GMT
Population: 100,000
Language: English
Religion: Christianity
Capital: St George's
Money: East Caribbean dollar = 100 cents
Weather: Tropical, with a dry season from January to May. In the wet season the temperature remains almost the same day and night.
National day: 7 February
National flag: Four triangles: two yellow top and bottom and two green on either side. Around the edge is a red border with three stars on the top edge and three on the bottom edge. In the centre is a red disc with a gold star, and a pod of nutmeg, the island's main product, sits in the green triangle nearest the flagpole.

- Grenada is nicknamed the Spice Island because of the nutmeg and other spices grown there.
- The Grand Etang, a fresh-water lake 530.35 metres above sea level on Grenada, sits in the crater of an extinct volcano.

Guadeloupe

Official name: Department of Guadeloupe
History: Guadeloupe has belonged to France for most of its history since the 17th century.
World location: Eastern Caribbean Sea. Guadeloupe is one of the Leeward Islands.
Area: 1,780 km^2
Local time: 4 hours behind GMT
Population: 340,000
Language: French; Creole is also spoken.
Religion: Christian (Roman Catholic)
Capital: Pointe-à-Pitre
Other major centre: Basse-Terre
Money: Franc = 100 centimes
Weather: Warm, with sea breezes

- The Caribs, who were living on the island before the Spanish arrived, named Guadeloupe *Karukera*, which means 'Isle of Beautiful Waters'. Present-day visitors agree with them and Guadeloupe is a popular holiday island for thousands of tourists every year.

Guatemala

Official name: Republic of Guatemala
History: A Spanish colony from the 16th century, Guatemala became independent in 1821.
World location: Central America, with its western coastline on the Pacific Ocean, and eastern coastline on the Caribbean Sea.
Area: 108,889 km^2
Local time: 6 hours behind GMT

Guatemala

Population: 8,680,000
Language: Spanish; local Indian Languages are also spoken.
Religion: Christian (mainly Roman Catholic)
Capital: Guatemala City
Other major centres: Quetzaltenango, Puerto Barrios, Mazatenango
Money: Quetzal = 100 centavos
Weather: Tropical, with little change in termperature. There is a wet season from May to October.
Main rivers: Motagua, Usumacinta
Main mountain ranges: Sierra Madre, Sierra de las Minas, Sierra de los Cuchumatanes
National day: 15 September
National flag: Three vertical stripes of blue, white, blue with the national coat of arms on the white stripe.

● The *quetzal* is the national symbol of Guatemala and is a beautiful tropical bird. The male quetzal has bright green wings, head and back and a deep red breast and under parts. It also has very long plumes on its wings and tail. The two middle tail plumes are often two metres long. The country's money and also its second largest city are named after the quetzal.

Guinea

Official name: Republic of Guinea
History: Guinea became a French colony at the end of the 19th century and became independent in 1958.
World location: West Africa, with its western coastline on the Atlantic Ocean
Area: 245,857 km²
Local time: GMT

Population: 5,070,000
Language: French; local languages are also spoken
Religion: The largest religious group are Moslem, next come followers of traditional local religions. There are a small number of Christians.
Capital: Conakry
Other major centres: Kankan, Labé, Kindia
Money: Guinea franc = 100 cents
Weather: Hot and humid on the coast, cooler and drier in the mountains
Main river: Niger
Main mountain range: Fouta Djalon
National day: 2 October
National flag: Three vertical stripes of red, yellow and green.

- Less than 2 per cent of the roads in Guinea have a tarmac or other hard surface, so many become very waterlogged and boggy in wet weather.
- In 1984 there was one television set in Guinea for every 840 people.

Guinea-Bissau

Official name: Republic of Guinea-Bissau
History: Guinea-Bissau became a Portuguese colony in the 15th century and remained under Portuguese control until 1974 when it became fully independent.
World location: West Africa, with its western coastline on the Atlantic Ocean
Area: 36,125 km^2
Local time: GMT
Population: 940,000

Guinea Bissau

Language: Portuguese is the official language; Crioulo is also spoken.
Religion: The largest religious group are Moslems. There are a small number of Christians.
Capital: Bissau
Money: Guinea-Bissau peso = 100 centavos
Weather: Hot, with a wet season from June to November
Main rivers: Cacheu, Mansoa, Geba
National day: 24 September
National flag: Two horizontal stripes of yellow and green. Next to the flagpole is a red rectangle with a black star.

- Guinea-Bissau was the oldest European colony in Africa. The first Portuguese sailors arrived there in 1446.

Guyana

Official name: Co-Operative Republic of Guyana
History: Originally a Dutch colony, Guyana became a British colony in the 19th Century and was granted independence in 1970.
World location: North-east of South America, with its northern coastline on the Atlantic Ocean
Area: 214,969 km²
Local time: 3 hours behind GMT
Population: 1,010,000
Language: English
Religion: The largest religious group is Christian, next comes the Hindu community, followed by a small number of Moslems.
Capital: Georgetown

Other major centres: New Amsterdam, Linden, Rose Hall

Money: Guyanese dollar = 100 cents

Weather: High humidity, with a rainy season from April to July and November to January. Sea breezes keep the temperature comfortable.

Main rivers: Essequibo, Courantyne, Mazaruni

Main mountain ranges: Pakaraima, Serra Acararai, Kanuku

National days: 23 February and 26 May

National flag: Guyana has an unusual flag. The background is green and there are two large triangles. The biggest runs from the edge next to the flagpole across to the other side; this is coloured yellow, with a white edge. Inside it is a smaller red triangle, edged in black.

- Many of the early explorers came to Guyana in search of the legendary land of El Dorado, which was supposed to be rich in gold. All they found was a dense tropical rainforest. Four-fifths of Guyana is covered with dense forest, which is the home of many exotic animals and birds, among them the largest species of Toucan – a bird famous for its huge beak.
- The world's largest spider also lives in Guyana. This is the Goliath bird-eating spider which is 266.7 mm long and weighs 122.2 g.

Haiti

Official name: Republic of Haiti

History: Originally a Spanish colony, Haiti became a French possession in the 18th century. The country became independent in 1804.

Haiti

World location: Caribbean Sea. Haiti occupies the western part of the island of Hispaniola which it shares with the Dominican Republic.
Area: 27,750 km²
Local time: 5 hours behind GMT (summer time 4 hours behind)
Population: 5,520,000
Language: French is the official language, but most people speak Creole.
Religion: Christian (Roman Catholic)
Capital: Port-au-Prince
Other major centres: Cap Haïtien, Gonaïves, Les Cayes
Money: Gourde = 100 centimes
Weather: Tropical. Cooler in the north. Rainy season May to September
Main river: Artibonite
Main mountain range: Massif de la Hotte
National day: 1 January
National flag: Two horizontal stripes of blue over red with the national coat of arms on a white panel in the centre.

- Most of the people on Haiti are of African origin and still follow African customs. Work on small farms is accompanied by the beating of drums. This mixture of work and play is known as a *combite*.
- One of the three ships with which Christopher Columbus made his famous voyage to the New World in 1492 was wrecked off the coast of Haiti in the winter of that year. The ship was named the *Santa Maria* and her anchor is preserved in the maritime museum in Port-au-Prince.

Honduras

Official name: Republic of Honduras
History: Honduras was a Spanish colony which became fully independent in 1838.
World location: Central America, with its coastline on the Pacific Ocean and eastern coastline on the Caribbean Sea
Area: 112,088 km²
Local time: 6 hours behind GMT
Population: 4,800,000
Language: Spanish
Religion: Christian (mainly Roman Catholic)
Capital: Tegucigalpa
Other major centres: San Pedro Sula, El Progresso, Choluteca
Money: Lempira = 100 centavos
Weather: Hot and humid on the coast, cooler in the hills
Main rivers: Patuca, Ulua
National day: 15 September
National flag: Three horizontal stripes of blue, white, blue. There are five blue stars in the centre of the white stripe.

- Honduras is the home of many rare and endangered animals like the black panther, the armadillo and the anteater.
- Honduras lies in the path of hurricanes. In 1974 one of these violent tropical storms caused the country's worst natural disaster in the twentieth century. Over 5,000 people were killed, and roads, crops and buildings were all severely damaged.

Hong Kong

Official name: Colony of Hong Kong

History: Hong Kong has been a British colony since the 19th century. Japan occupied the colony during the Second World War. Hong Kong is due to be returned to China in 1997.

World location: East Asia, off the south-east coast of China

Area: 1,068 km^2

Local time: 8 hours ahead of GMT

Population: 5,680,000

Language: English and Chinese (Cantonese dialect)

Religion: Mainly Buddhist

Money: Hong Kong dollar = 100 cents

Weather: Summers are hot and humid, winters warmer and drier.

National flag: The flag of Hong Kong is the British Blue Ensign with a white disc bearing the colony's coat of arms.

- Hong Kong has probably more forms of public transport than any other city in the world. As well as buses and trains, there are many different ways of travelling round the colony by water. On average ten million passenger journeys are made every day.
- The government of Hong Kong is the world's biggest landlord. About 2,500,000 people live in public housing.
- 37,000 people in Hong Kong live permanently on boats.
- Hong Kong is the world's leading exporter of clothing, toys and watches.
- There are more than 1,250,000 people in full-time education in Hong Kong.

Hungary

Official name: Republic of Hungary
History: Hungary first became a republic in 1918. At the start of the Second World War Hungary sided with Germany, but it was occupied by Germany in 1944 until liberated by the USSR in 1945, when the Communist republic was formed. In 1989 the Communist government was replaced by a more popular government.
World location: Eastern Europe
Area: 93,036 km^2
Local time: 1 hour ahead of GMT (summer time 2 hours ahead)
Population: 10,600,000
Language: Hungarian (Magyar)
Religion: Christian
Capital: Budapest
Other major centres: Debrecen, Miskolc, Szeged, Pecs, Györ
Money: Forint = 100 filler
Weather: Warm summers, cold winters
Main river: Duna (Danube) and its tributaries
Main mountain ranges: Cserhát, Mát, Bükk
National day: 4 April
National flag: Three horizontal stripes of red, white and green.

- The man who invented the Rubik cube in 1975, Professor Erno Rubik, is Hungarian.
- One person in five in Hungary lives in Budapest.
- The rivers and lakes of Hungary have an important fishing industry with an annual catch approaching 40,000 tonnes of freshwater fish.

Iceland

Official name: Republic of Iceland
History: Iceland was independent until the 13th century when it became part of Norway and later Denmark. It became a fully independent republic once again in 1944.
World location: North Atlantic Ocean
Area: 103,000 km²
Local time: GMT
Population: 250,000
Language: Icelandic
Religion: Christian (mainly Lutheran)
Capital: Reykjavik
Other major centres: Kopavogur, Akureyri, Hafnarfjordur
Money: Icelandic Krona = 100 aurar
Weather: Cool, with long winters and short summers
Main rivers: Thjorsa, Skjalfandafljot
National day: 17 June
National flag: Blue, with a white-bordered red cross.

- Iceland has been named the 'land of frost and fires', because on the island glaciers are found right next to hot springs and volcanoes.
- Hot underground water is used to heat homes, factories, public buildings and outdoor swimming pools in Iceland.
- Reykjavik lies just below the Arctic Circle and is the most northerly capital in the world.
- The Icelandic parliament, the *Althing*, is the world's oldest surviving parliament. It was founded in the year 930.
- Iceland is also one of the so-called 'lands of the midnight sun'. Since it lies so far north there is daylight almost twenty-four hours a day at the height of the summer in

the middle of June. In the middle of winter the darkness is almost as long.

- Icelandic women do not change their surnames when they marry. Their last name is their mother's first name followed by the word *dottir* 'daughter'

- Living in Iceland is good for you, if health figures are anything to judge by! On average men and women in Iceland live longer than the inhabitants of any other country.

- The name Reykjavik means 'Bay of Smokes'.

India

History: India has one of the oldest recorded civilizations on earth. The country came under British control in the 18th century and was granted independence in 1947.

World location: South Asia. The Indian peninsula has the Arabian Sea to the west and the Bay of Bengal to the east.

Area: 3,287,263 km^2

Local Time: 5½ hours ahead of GMT

Population: 796,600,000

Language: Hindi and English; local languages are also spoken by millions of people in different states.

Religion: Mainly Hindu; Moslem, Sikh, Christian, Buddhist communities as well

Capital: New Delhi

Other major centres: Bombay, Calcutta, Madras, Bangalore, Hyderabad, Ahmedabad

Money: Rupee = 100 paisa

Weather: Great variety from very cold in the mountains of the north to tropical in the south

India

Main rivers: Ganges, Brahmaputra, Sutlej, Narmeda, Tapti

Main mountain ranges: Himalayas, Gravalti, Sappura Vindhya, Western Ghats

National day: 26 January

National flag: Three horizontal stripes of orange, white and green. In the middle of the white stripe is an ancient emblem shaped like a wheel. This is called a *Chakra*, meaning 'Wheel of Law'.

- Fourteen major languages are spoken in India as well as a further 1,000 minor languages and local dialects.
- The singer Miss Lata Mangeshker has probably made more records than anybody else. She has sung on over 30,000 records in twenty Indian languages.
- The Taj Mahal in the Indian city of Agra is regarded as one of the most beautiful buildings in the world. It was built by the Indian ruler Shah Jahan in memory of his wife. The white marble building took twenty-one years to build and employed 20,000 workmen. The tall minarets that stand at each corner were designed to fall outwards if any disaster should happen, to prevent them from toppling on to the main building.
- About 575,000,000 people in India follow the Hindu religion. They believe in *Ahinsa*, a principal that prevents them from harming any living creature. Hindus hold cows sacred as a result of this and cows are allowed to wander freely through the streets in many parts of India. For the same reason no Hindu will eat beef and many eat no meat at all.

Indonesia

Official name: Republic of Indonesia

History: Indonesia became a Dutch colony in the 17th century. Japan invaded the islands during the Second World War. In 1945 the country became independent.

World location: South-east Asia. Indonesia consists of 13,700 islands, 6,000 of which are inhabited, off the mainland of south-east Asia.

Area: 1,919,400 km²

Local time: West zone 7 hours ahead of GMT, central zone 8 hours ahead of GMT, Eastern zone 9 hours ahead of GMT

Population: 174,950,000

Language: Bahasa Indonesian; Dutch is also spoken.

Religion: Mainly Moslem; some Christians and Hindus

Capital: Jakarta

Other major centres: Surabaya, Semarang, Bandung, Palembang, Medan, Ujung Pandang

Money: Rupiah = 100 sen

Weather: Hot and rainy, cooler in the mountain areas

Main rivers: Kapuas, Digul, Barito

Main mountain ranges: Bukit, Barisan Pegungungan Jayawijaya

National day: 17 August

National flag: Two horizontal stripes of red and white.

- There are sixty active volcanos in Indonesia. Although there is always a risk that they might erupt, Indonesians like living near volcanos because volcanic ash makes the soil fertile for growing crops.
- Traditional Indonesian houses are built on stilts 1.8 metres high. The space underneath is used to house cattle or chickens.

Indonesia

- The Indonesian stick insect is the longest insect in the world. Some have measured as much as 330 mm overall.

Iran

Official name: Islamic Repulic of Iran
History: The ancient kingdom of Persia changed its name to Iran in 1935. The country was a monarchy ruled by the Shahs until 1979, when the last Shah left the country after widespread unrest. Ayatollah Khomeini established an Islamic republic later in the same year.
World location: Western Asia with its northern coastline on the Caspian Sea and southern coastline on the Persian Gulf
Area: 1,648,000 km^2
Local time: 3½ hours ahead of GMT
Population: 52,520,000
Language: Farsi (Persian); local languages are spoken as well.
Religion: Moslem
Capital: Tehran
Other major centres: Esfahan, Mashad, Tabriz, Shiraz, Ahvaz, Abadan
Money: Rial = 100 dinars
Weather: Very hot in the south, cooler and dry in the central desert areas. The shores of the Black Sea are sub-tropical.
Main rivers: Karun, Safid, Atrak, Karkheh
Main mountain ranges: Elburz Mountains, Zagros Mountains
National day: 11 February
National flag: Three horizontal stripes of green, white

and red. The national emblem appears in red in the centre of the white stripe.

- Iran is the oldest country in the world. It has been independent since the 6th century BC.
- The earliest windmills yet discovered have been found in Iran. They were first put to use grinding corn in the 7th century AD.
- The main foods eaten in Iran are rice and bread (some of which looks like and is named 'Elephant's ears'). Traditional Iranian dishes include *abgusht* (a thick vegetable and bean soup), and *dolmeh* (vegetables stuffed with meat and rice). *Dough* is a popular drink made from yoghurt.

Iraq

Official name: Republic of Iraq
History: From the 16th century Iraq was part of the Ottoman Empire, centred on Turkey. The country became a fully independent kingdom in 1932 and a republic was formed in 1958.
World location: Middle East, with its western coastline on the Persian Gulf
Area: 434,924 km^2
Local time: 3 hours ahead of GMT (summer time 4 hours ahead)
Population: 17,660,000
Language: Arabic
Religion: Moslem
Capital: Baghdad
Other major centres: Basrah, Mosul, Kirkuk, Najaf
Money: Iraqi dinar = 1,000 fils

Iraq

Weather: Very hot and dry in desert areas. Humid near the coast. Highland areas have cold, damp winters.
Main rivers: Tigris, Euphrates
Main mountain range: Kurdistan Mountains
National day: 17 July
National flag: Three horizontal stripes of red, white and black. There are three green stars on the white stripe.

- Iraq was the centre for one of the earliest civilizations. The world's oldest surviving map was drawn in Iraq at about 3,800 BC. It shows the path of the River Euphrates.
- In the ancient world what we call Iraq was known as Mesopotamia, a name that comes from the Greek words meaning 'between the rivers'. The two rivers are the Tigris and Euphrates, between which lies the fertile land where the early civilizations in Iraq developed.
- The ancient city of Ur, which once stood in southern Iraq, housed the oldest known collection of wild animals. This dated back to about 2097 BC.
- Eight out of every ten dates eaten in the world are grown in Iraq. The country grows 100,000 tonnes of dates each year.

Ireland

Official name: Republic of Ireland
History: Ireland has been independent of the UK since 1921.
World location: North-east Atlantic Ocean. The country occupies the main part of the island of Ireland off the west coast of Europe.
Area: 70,283 km²
Local time: GMT (summer time 1 hour ahead of GMT)
Population: 3,540,000

Language: Irish is the official language; English is the
second official language.
Religion: Christian (Roman Catholic)
Capital: Dublin
Other major centres: Cork, Limerick, Galway,
Waterford
Money: Irish pound = 100 pence
Weather: Mild; rainfall is lowest along the eastern coast
Main rivers: Shannon, Suir, Boyne
Main mountain ranges: Macgillicuddy's Reeks,
Wicklow Mountains
National day: 17 March
National flag: Three vertical stripes of green, white and
orange.

- Hurling, the national game in Ireland, is one of the oldest
  games in the world, dating back thousands of years.
- According to Irish traditions there are no snakes in the
  country because St Patrick, the patron saint of Ireland
  banished them all.
- In the middle of the 19th century a terrible famine struck
  Ireland when the potato crop failed. Hundreds of
  thousands of people died of hunger and disease and
  about 1,500,000 Irish people went to live overseas,
  many to America. As a result of this catastrophe the
  population of Ireland was reduced by almost a half.

Israel

Official name: State of Israel
History: The State of Israel was established in 1948.
World location: Middle East, with its western coastline
on the Mediterranean Sea and an outlet to the Red Sea
in the south.

Israel

Area: 21,946 km^2
Local time: 2 hours ahead of GMT (summer time 3 hours ahead)
Population: 4,430,000
Language: Hebrew and Arabic are the official languages.
Religion: Jewish; smaller numbers of Moslems and Christians
Capital: Jerusalem
Other major centres: Tel-Aviv, Jaffa, Haifa, Ramat Gan
Money: Shekel = 100 agorot
Weather: Hot, dry summers and mild rainy winters
Main rivers: Jordan, Quishon
Main mountain range: Mountains of Judea
National day: 21 April
National flag: White with narrow blue horizontal stripes close to the top and bottom edges. In the centre are two triangles forming the shape of a star. This is known as the Star of David, named after King David, the Jewish king whose story is told in the Bible and who ruled about 3,000 years ago.

- The Israel painted frog is one of the rarest in the world. Since its discovery in 1940, only five have ever been seen.
- Unmarried Jewish women in Israel have to spend two years serving in the country's armed forces.
- The national dish in Israel is *steak im pitta*, thick slices of steak served in Arab bread with vegetables and a hot chilli sauce.

Italy

Official name: Italian Republic

History: The history of Italy dates far back into ancient times. The Roman Empire was founded in Italy and in the middle ages powerful city states grew up in the country. Italy became a republic in 1946.

World location: Southern Europe. The Italian peninsula is surrounded by sea on the west, east and south. There are also several islands which form part of the country, the largest of these being Sicily and Sardinia.

Area: 301,268 km²

Local time: 1 hour ahead of GMT (summer time 2 hours ahead)

Population: 57,440,000

Language: Italian

Religion: Christian (Roman Catholic)

Capital: Rome

Other major centres: Milan, Naples, Turin, Genoa, Palermo, Bologna, Florence

Money: Lira = 100 centesimi

Weather: Hot summers, mild winters, with cooler weather and high rainfall in the north

Main rivers: Po, Tiber, Arno, Volturno

Main mountain ranges: Appenines, Alps

National day: 2 June

National flag: Three vertical stripes of green, white and red.

- In the city of Venice most transport takes place by water. The traditional Venetian craft is a long, slender boat called a *gondola*, which is propelled with long paddles.
- Venice is also the home of the world's oldest surviving zoo, which was built in 1752 by the Holy Roman Emperor Franz I for his wife.
- Different regions in Italy, like those in France, have

become world famous for certain special foods or recipes. Bologna is famous for its sausages, Parma has given the world *prosciutto* (dried and salted ham), and the famous Italian soup called *minestrone* originated in Milan.

- The earliest examples of false teeth have been found in Italian tombs that date back to 700 BC. Some of the teeth were even designed so that they could be removed from the mouth, like modern dentures. Others were fixed in place permanently.
- The Italian flag was designed by the French emperor Napoleon Bonaparte.
- The City of Pisa is famous for its Leaning Tower. When building work started on this in 1173 the tower stood upright, but the foundations were not strong enough and it tilted 4.3 metres out of the perpendicular, which is how it has stayed for hundreds of years.
- Near the Leaning Tower of Pisa is the Campo Santo, a cemetery that was also built in the 12th century, using earth from the Holy Land.
- The great Gothic cathedral in Milan is the third largest church in Europe and has 4,000 statues. Building work on this lasted from 1386 until the 19th century.

Jamaica

History: Jamaica was a British colony from the 17th century until it became independent in 1962.
World location: Caribbean Sea. Jamaica is about 150 km south of Cuba
Area: 10,991 km^2
Local time: 5 hours behind GMT
Population: 2,450,000
Language: English

Religion: Christian (mainly Protestant)
Capital: Kingston
Other major centres: Spanish Town, Montego Bay,
May Pen, Mandeville
Money: Jamaican dollar = 100 cents
Weather: Tropical. Sea breezes keep the coastal areas
comfortable while the higher ground inland is cooler and
less humid.
Main river: Black River
Main mountain range: Blue Mountains
National day: First Monday in August
National flag: Yellow diagonal cross dividing flag into
green triangles top and bottom and black triangles on
either side.

- The earliest known inhabitants of Jamaica were the
  Arawak Indians, who lived on the island from about the
  year 1000. The Arawaks called Jamaica *Xaymaca*,
  which means 'land of wood and water'.
- About half of the land in Jamaica is over 300 m above
  sea level.
- The giant swallow-tail butterfly is unique to Jamaica. This
  huge butterfly, which measures 150 cm across its wings,
  is found nowhere else in the world.
- Seafood is very popular in Jamaica, especially shrimp
  and swordfish. A traditional dish called Stand and Go is
  made of codfish cakes.

Japan

History: For over 2,000 years Japan has been ruled by
the same family of emperors.
World location: North-east Asia. Japan is made up of a
chain of islands lying off the north-east coast of Asia.

Japan

Area: 377,800 km^2
Local time: 1 hour ahead of GMT
Population: 122,610,000
Language: Japanese
Religion: Shintoism and Buddhism
Capital: Tokyo
Other major centres: Yokohama, Osaka, Nagoya, Sapporo, Kyoto
Money: Yen = 100 sen
Weather: South hot and rainy in summer, mild in winter; the north has warm summers but long, cold winters
Main rivers: Tone, Ishikari, Shinano
Main mountain range: Hida
National day: 29 April
National flag: White with a large red disc representing the sun; the Japanese name for Japan is Nippon, which means the 'source of the sun'.

- The western name for Japan developed from the name given to the country by the Venetian traveller Marco Polo, who journeyed across Asia in the 13th century. He called it *Cipanago*.
- Japan was the home of the world's oldest recorded human being, a man called Shigechiyo Izumi, who lived to be 120 years old.
- Sumo wrestling, the national sport in Japan, dates from about 23 BC. All Sumo wrestlers are heavy but the heaviest on record weighed 252 kg. However he was born in Hawaii.
- The Japanese are great eaters of fish, and eat more fish per person than any other nation on earth. *Sushi*, a mixture of rice, raw fish and vegetables, is a national dish. *Miso* (a paste made from soya beans) is served with many Japanese recipes. The country's most popular drink is *sake*, made from rice.
- Japan has the best selling newspaper in the world, the

Ymiuri Shimbun, which has sales reaching 14,000,000 copies in a single day.
- The railway network in Japan is the busiest in the world. Roughly 13,850,000 travel on it every day.

Jordan

Official name: Hashemite Kingdom of Jordan
History: At the end of the First World War in 1918, Jordan, which had previously been part of the Ottoman Empire controlled by Turkey, came under British protection. In 1946 Jordan became an independent kingdom.
World location: Middle East
Area: 97,740 km^2
Local time: 3 hours ahead of GMT (summer time 2 hours ahead)
Population: 3,940,000
Language: Arabic
Religion: Moslem
Capital: Amman
Other major centres: Zarqa, Irbid
Money: Jordanian dinar = 1,000 fils
Weather: Hot and dry
Main river: Jordan
National day: 25 May
National flag: Three horizontal stripes of black, white and green. On the side nearest the flagpole is a red triangle with a white star.

- Jerusalem is a very old city. It is sacred to Jews, Moslems and Christians and contains the ruins of many ancient buildings. The city also has the remains of the

113

world's earliest known dams which were built of stone as long ago as 3200 BC.

- The Dead Sea, which lies on the border of Jordan and Israel, is seven times saltier than the ocean. As a result it is very difficult to swim underwater. In fact the easiest thing to do is to lie on your back and enjoy the sunshine or read a book! The shoreline of the Dead Sea is the lowest land in the world, lying 395 metres below sea level.

Kenya

Official name: Republic of Kenya
History: Until its independence in 1963 Kenya had been governed by the UK since the 19th century.
World location: East central Africa, with its Eastern coastline on the Indian Ocean
Area: 582,600 km²
Local time: 3 hours ahead of GMT
Population: 23,880,000
Language: Kiswahili is the official language; several local languages are spoken as well. English is sometimes used for business.
Religion: Mainly Christian
Capital: Nairobi
Other major centres: Mombasa, Kisumu, Nakuru, Machakos
Money: Kenya shilling = 100 cents
Weather: Hot in the coastal lowlands, cooler in the higher plateau areas
Main rivers: Tana, Umba, Athi
Main mountain range: Aberdare Mountains
National day: 12 December

National flag: Three horizontal stripes of black, red and green, with narrow white stripes above and below the red. In the centre is a long oval shield in front of two crossed spears.

- Nairobi was first used as a watering point. Only a hundred years later it became the Kenyan capital.
- In spite of Kenya's position on the Equator, where the weather is frequently very hot, the country's highest mountain is snow-capped all year round. Mount Kenya itself has twelve small glaciers.
- In parts of Kenya the baobab tree grows to an enormous size. This strange looking tree has short branches and a very thick trunk, which is used for storing water. Some of the oldest baobab trees now have hollow trunks and some have been turned into shelters or small homes.

Kiribati

Official name: Republic of Kiribati
History: Kiribati became a British colony at the end of the 19th century. The islands gained independence in 1979.
World location: South-west Pacific Ocean. Kiribati is made up of three groups of small coral islands and one volcanic island, spread over a large area.
Area: 717 km^2
Local time: 12 hours ahead of GMT
Population: 70,000
Language: Kiribati; English is also spoken
Religion: Christian
Capital: Tarawa
Money: Australian dollar = 100 cents

Kiribati

Weather: Warm and comfortable. The rainy season lasts from December to February.
National day: 12 July
National flag: Red, with blue and white wavy lines at the bottom. In the centre is a golden rising sun and a flying frigate bird.

- The coral rock of which the island is made has a covering of sand and light soil that is only 2 metres deep. The soil is so poor that little grows except scrub and coconut palms.
- The people of Kiribati are very experienced sailors. They can steer by the stars without the need for navigational instruments and some are even able to find their way by the changing smell of the sea.

Korea, North

Official name: Democratic People's Republic of Korea
History: At one time Korea was a kingdom, controlled for a long period by China. In 1895 it became independent. Ten years later the country was occupied by Japan. After the defeat of Japan at the end of the Second World War in 1945, Korea was divided into two zones: North Korea and South Korea. North Korea was the area occupied by the USSR at the end of the war. It became a Communist republic in 1948.
World location: Eastern Asia. The northern part of the Korean peninsula western coastline lies on the Yellow Sea, the eastern coastline on the Sea of Japan.
Area: 120,538 km²
Local time: 9 hours ahead of GMT
Population: 21,900,000
Language: Korean

Religion: Confucianism, Buddhism
Capital: Pyongyang
Other major centres: Hamhung, Chongjin, Kimchaek, Wonsan
Money: North Korean won = 100 chon
Weather: Cold. Dry winters and hot, humid, rainy summers.
Main rivers: Imjin, Ch'ongch'on, Yalu
Main mountain range: Nangnim Sanmaek
National day: 8 September
National flag: Horizontal stripes of blue, red and blue separated by narrow bands of white. In the centre of the red stripe is a white disc with a red star.

- Films are popular in North Korea, and most of those seen are provided free of charge by a large number of mobile cinemas that travel round the country putting on film shows.

Korea, South

Official name: Republic of South Korea
History: Until the end of the Second World War the two Koreas were joined. South Korea was created at the end of the war from the southern area of Korea occupied by the USA.
World location: Eastern Asia. It is the southern part of the Korean peninsula, with its western coastline on the Yellow Sea and eastern coastline on the Sea of Japan.
Area: 99,022 km^2
Local time: 9 hours ahead of GMT (summer time 10 hours ahead.
Population: 41,970,000
Language: Korean

Korea, South

Religion: Confucianism, Buddhism; small Christian community
Capital: Seoul
Other major centres: Pusan, Taegu, Inchon, Kwangchu
Money: South Korean won = 100 chon
Weather: Cold, dry winters and hot, humid, rainy summers
Main rivers: Han, Naktong, Kum, Somjin
National day: 15 August
National flag: From the end of the 15th century to the beginning of the 20th century Confucianism was the official religion in Korea and this is reflected in the flag of South Korea today. The background of the flag is white. In the centre is a disc of red and blue divided by a wavy line, which is a religious symbol representing two forces of nature called *yin* and *yang*. In each corner of the flag are sets of short black lines. These are called trigrams. Again they are religious symbols with many meanings. On the flag they represent the four elements:

≡≡ air   ≡ ≡ fire   ≡≡ earth   ≡ ≡ water

● When Buddhism was at its height in Korea about 500 years ago, the Haein-sa Temple near Taegu collected a library of over 80,000 wooden blocks. These were all carved by hand and were used for printing Buddhist scriptures.

Kuwait

Official name: State of Kuwait
History: Kuwait came under British protection at the end of the 19th century. The country became fully

independent again in 1961. In the summer of 1990
Kuwait was invaded by Iraq. This was widely
condemned by many countries around the world and
led to United Nations sanctions against Iraq to force the
invaders to retreat.

World location: Middle East, with its eastern coastline
on the Persian Gulf
Area: 17,818 km²
Local time: 3 hours ahead of GMT
Population: 1,960,000
Language: Arabic
Religion: Moslem
Capital: Kuwait City
Money: Kuwait dinar = 1,000 fils
Weather: Hot and humid
National day: 25 February
National flag: Three horizontal stripes of green, white
and red. Next to the flagpole is a black triangle with the
point cut off. This shape is known as a trapezium.

- There are no lakes or rivers in Kuwait, which is almost
  entirely desert. Water is provided by purifying sea water
  in a process known as distillation and then mixing this
  with water drawn from wells.

Laos

Official name: Lao People's Democratic Republic
History: Laos came under French protection at the end
of the 19th century. The Japanese occupied the country
in the Second World War. Laos became independent
from France in 1949. The country was made a
Communist republic, following twenty years of civil war,
in 1973.

Laos

World location: South-east Asia
Area: 236,800 km²
Local time: 7 hours ahead of GMT
Population: 3,870,000
Language: Lao is the official language
Religion: Buddhism has the largest following, traditional local religions are also practised.
Capital: Vientiane
Other major centres: Luang Prabang, Pakse, Savannakhet
Money: New Kip = 100 at
Weather: Warm and humid, with a monsoon period from May to October
Main river: Mekong
Main mountain range: Annamitic Range
National day: 2 December
National flag: Three horizontal stripes of red, blue and red. The blue stripe is twice the width of the red ones and in its centre is a large white disc.

- At one time the songs of travelling ballad singers were often the only way of hearing the news in Laos.
- The Khone Falls in Laos are the widest waterfalls in the world, measuring 10.8 km from one side to the other.
- Laos is well known for its very hot curries and dishes made with chillies. Food is frequently eaten raw. Special Lao dishes include ant's eggs, stuffed frogs and *som Khay*, Laotian caviar.

Lebanon

Official name: Republic of Lebanon
History: Lebanon was part of the Ottoman Empire centred on Turkey until the end of the First World War in

1918. The country was then controlled by France until 1941, when it became independent. For the last ten years there has been fighting between various religious and political groups in Lebanon, and at different times troops from other countries have occupied a number of areas of the country.

World location: Middle East, with its western coastline on the Mediterranean Sea

Area: 10,452 km²

Local time: 2 hours ahead of GMT (summer time 3 hours ahead).

Population: 2,830,000

Language: Arabic; French and English are spoken as well

Religion: Moslem and Christian

Capital: Beirut

Other major centres: Tripoli, Zahlé, Sidon, Tyre

Money: Lebanese pound = 100 piastres

Weather: The lowlands along the coast have hot, humid summers and cool, damp winters. The mountains are cooler, with heavy snow in winter.

Main river: Nahr-al-Litani (Leontes)

Main mountain ranges: Lebanon Range, Anti-Lebanon Range

National day: 22 November

National flag: Three horizontal stripes of red, white and red. The white stripe is twice the width of the red ones. In its centre is a green tree, a cedar of Lebanon, the country's symbol.

● Although the cedar of Lebanon is the country's national symbol there are fewer than ten groves of these great trees left in the country.

Lesotho

Official name: Kingdom of Lesotho
History: Lesotho came under British protection in the 19th century. It became fully independent in 1966.
World location: Southern Africa. Lesotho is completely surrounded by South Africa.
Area: 30,355 km²
Local time: 2 hours ahead of GMT
Population: 1,680,000
Language: Sesotho and English are the official languages.
Religion: Christian
Capital: Maseru
Money: Maloti = 100 lisente
Weather: Mild and pleasant, with cold snowy winters in the highlands
Main rivers: Orange, Caledon
Main mountain range: Drakensberg
National day: 4 October
National flag: Three diagonal stripes of white, blue and green. The white stripe is twice the width of the others. In the upper corner next to the flagpole is a brown shield.

- Lesotho has been nicknamed the 'Roof of Africa' and the 'Switzerland of Southern Africa' because of its beautiful mountain scenery.
- So much of Lesotho is mountainous that nowhere in the country is below 1,380 metres above sea level. This makes Lesotho the country with the highest 'lowest point' on earth.
- In Lesotho wealth is measured by the number of cattle a person owns. Cattle are often used instead of money for payment.

- Large areas of Lesotho are given over to pasture. Wool and mohair are two of the country's main exports.
- Women do much of the farming and production of food in Lesotho, because many of the men are away working in mines in South Africa.

Liberia

Official name: Republic of Liberia
History: Liberia was founded in the 19th century by freed American slaves.
World location: West Africa, with its western coastline on the Atlantic Ocean
Area: 111,370 km^2
Local time: GMT
Population: 2,510,000
Language: English; local languages are also spoken.
Religion: Christian
Capital: Monrovia
Other major centres: Buchanan, Greenville, Harper
Money: Liberian dollar = 100 cents
Weather: Hot and humid
Main rivers: St Paul, St John, Cess
Main mountain range: Guinea Highlands
National day: 26 July
National flag: The Liberian flag has close connections with the flag of the USA. There are six red and five white alternating horizontal stripes, similar to the thirteen red and white stripes on the US flag. In the upper corner next to the flagpole is a blue square on which sits a white star.

- Liberia is the oldest independent republic in West Africa.
- Liberia has the largest registered merchant navy in the

world. Many of the ships are owned by foreign companies who register their ships there because it is very convenient and less expensive than registration in most other countries. Ten years ago the number of ships registered in Liberia was almost one for every 660 people in the country.

Libya

Official name: Socialist People's Libyan Arab Jamahiriya

History: From the 16th century until the 20th century Libya was controlled by Turkey. In 1912 Italy occupied the country. From 1942 it was governed by France and the UK, until it became an independent kingdom in 1951. The king was overthrown in 1969 and a republic was declared.

World location: North Africa, with its northern coastline on the Mediterranean Sea

Area: 1,759,540 km²

Local time: 1 hour ahead of GMT (summer time 2 hours ahead)

Population: 4,230,000

Language: Arabic

Religion: Moslem

Capital: Tripoli

Other major centres: Benghazi, Misurata

Money: Libyan dinar = 1,000 dirhams

Weather: Dry and hot in the desert areas of the south, milder and wetter on the coast

Main river: Wadi-al-Farigh

Main mountain ranges: Jabal as-Sawda, Al Kufrah, Al Haruj al-Aswad

National day: 1 September

National flag: The Libyan flag is plain green.

- Before oil was discovered, Libya was a very poor country. Today it has the highest income per person in Africa.
- The highest shade temperature anywhere on earth was recorded at El Aziza in Libya in 1922, when the thermometer rose to 58°C.

Liechtenstein

Official name: Principality of Liechtenstein
History: Liechtenstein has been a principality since the 14th century.
World location: Central Europe
Area: 160 km²
Local time: 1 hour ahead of GMT (summer time 2 hours)
Population: 30,000
Language: German
Religion: Christian (mainly Roman Catholic)
Capital: Vaduz
Money: Swiss franc = 100 centimes
Weather: Alpine, warm summers, cold winters in higher areas
Main river: Rhein (Rhine)
Main mountain range: Alps
National day: 15 August
National flag: Two horizontal stripes of blue and red. In the upper corner next to the flagpole is the prince's crown in gold.

- Prince Hartmann of Liechtenstein, who lived in the 17th century, was the father of twenty-four children.

Liechtenstein

- Liechtenstein has had no army since 1868.
- One-third of the population of Liechtenstein consists of workers from other countries.
- Sixty years ago seventy out of every hundred working people in Liechtenstein worked on the land. Today that number has fallen to just three in every hundred.

Luxembourg

Official name: Grand Duchy of Luxembourg
History: Luxembourg was part of the Holy Roman Empire until the French conquered it at the end of the 18th century. In 1815 it became independent.
World location: Western Europe
Area: 2,586 km^2
Local time: 1 hour ahead of GMT (summer time 2 hours ahead)
Population: 370,000
Language: Luxemburgish; French, German and English are also spoken.
Religion: Christian (mainly Roman Catholic)
Capital: Luxembourg
Other major centres: Esch-Alzette, Differdange, Dudelange
Money: Luxembourg franc = 100 centimes
Weather: Cool summers, mild winters in lowland areas. The uplands have cold, snowy winters.
Main rivers: Mosel, Sûre, Our
Main mountain range: Ardennes
National day: 23 June
National flag: Three horizontal stripes of red, white and light blue.

- Luxembourg is one of the world's leading car-owning

countries. In 1980 it ranked third in the world with almost 481 cars to every 1,000 people.

Macao

History: Macao has been a Portuguese colony since the 16th century. In 1999 it will be returned to China.
World location: Eastern Asia. Macao consists of a peninsula and two islands off the southern coast of China 60 km west of Hong Kong
Area: 17 km^2
Local Time: 8 hours ahead of GMT
Population: 440,000
Language: Portuguese; Chinese (Cantonese) is widely spoken as well
Religion: Mainly Buddhist
Money: Pataca = 100 avos
Weather: Hot and humid

- In 1948 the first hijacking of an aircraft took place between Macao and Hong Kong when a group of Chinese bandits seized control of a flying-boat. The aircraft crashed during the struggle between the hijackers and the crew and the police only discovered what had happened when the leader of the gang was in hospital recovering.

Madagascar

Official name: Democratic Republic of Madagascar
History: Madagascar was a French colony from the end of the 19th century until it became fully independent in 1960.
World location: Western Indian Ocean. The country lies on the island of Madagascar off the east African coast of Mozambique
Area: 587,041 km^2
Local time: 3 hours ahead of GMT
Population: 11,240,000
Language: Malagasy; French and English are also spoken
Religion: Christian and traditional local religions
Capital: Antananarivo
Other major centres: Toamasina, Mahajanga, Fianarantsoa
Money: Madagascar franc = 100 centimes
Weather: Hot on coast, cooler inland. Mountains cause heavy rainfall in the east, but the west is much drier.
Main rivers: Ikopa, Mania, Manoky
Main mountain ranges: Massif du Tsaratanan, Ankaratra
National day: 26 June
National flag: Two horizontal stripes of red and green. Next to the flagpole is a vertical white stripe.

- The largest eggs laid by a known animal are those of the extinct Elephant bird that once lived on Madagascar. A freshly laid egg probably weighed 12.24 kg.
- In the 17th and 18th centuries Madagascar was a popular haven for sea pirates, including the notorious Captain Kidd. At one period the pirates set up their own system of government, but it lasted for only a short time.

Malawi

Official name: Republic of Malawi
History: Malawi came under British protection at the end of the 19th century. The country became independent in 1964.
World location: Central Africa
Area: 118,484 km^2
Local time: 2 hours ahead of GMT
Population: 7,750,000
Language: Chichewa and English
Religion: Christian
Capital: Lilongwe
Other major centres: Blantyre, Mzuzu, Zomba
Money: Malawi Kwacha = 100 tambala
Weather: Tropical, with a wet season from November to April
Main river: Shire
National day: 6 July
National flag: Three horizontal stripes of black, red and green, with a red rising sun in the centre of the black stripe.

- Many of the 200 species of fish found in Malawi are found nowhere else in the world.
- Lake Malawai is the world's tenth largest lake and the third largest in Africa. It covers an area of 29,600 km^2, making it almost one and a half times the size of Wales.

Malaysia

Official name: Federation of Malaysia
History: The countries forming Malaysia were under British protection until they became an independent federation in 1963. Singapore left the federation in 1965.
World location: South-east Asia. Malaysia consists of the southern part of the Kra peninsula and the territories of Sabah and Sarawak on the north coast of the island of Borneo.
Area: 329,749 km^2
Local time: 8 hours ahead of GMT
Population: 16,920,000
Language: Malay; Chinese, Tamil and Iban are also spoken
Religion: Moslem and Buddhist
Capital: Kuala Lumpur
Other major centres: Ipoh, Pinang, Johor Bahru, Kuala Terrengganu
Money: Malaysian ringgit (dollar) = 100 sen
Weather: Humid; hotter in Peninsular Malaysia than in Sarawak or Sabah. The whole country is affected by monsoons.
Main rivers: Pahang, Kelantan
Main mountain range: Trengganu Highlands
National day: 31 August
National flag: Fourteen horizontal stripes of alternating red and white. In the upper corner next to the flagpole is a blue panel with a gold crescent and a gold star with fourteen points. The fourteen points of the star and the fourteen stripes represent the fourteen states that originally made up the Federation of Malaysia. The flag remains unchanged even though Singapore left the federation.

● Kite flying is popular with both adults and children in

Malaysia. The *wau* (kite) comes in different shapes and sizes and is beautifully decorated. Often a bow-shaped device is attached to give the kite a high-pitched sound when it is in flight. The *wau-butan* or moon-kite, so-called because of its crescent shape, is the largest type of kite flown in Malaysia and the most popular.

- *Wayang Kulit* (Shadow Plays) in Malaysia are exciting and great fun. The puppet figures used in the plays are carved from buffalo hide, painted and fitted with long handles, with usually at least one moving arm. Performances take place behind a large white cotton screen, with the figures held behind the screen. A hanging light casts a moving shadow. The audience sit or stand on the other side of the screen watching the shadows and listening to the story as it is performed. The story is told by the *Tok Dalang* (Father of the Mysteries), who varies his voice as he plays different characters.

- Malaysia is the world's leading exporter of tin, natural rubber and palm oil. It also produces a quarter of the world's paper.

Maldives

Official name: Republic of the Maldives
History: The Maldive islands came under British protection in 1887. They gained complete independence in 1965.
World location: Northern Indian Ocean. The Maldives consist of 1,200 islands in 12 groups 700 km south-west of Sri Lanka.
Area: 298 km^2
Local time: 5 hours ahead of GMT
Population: 200,000
Language: Divehi

Maldives

Religion: Moslem
Capital: Malé
Money: Maldivian rufiyaa = 100 laari
Weather: Very warm and humid
National day: 26 July
National flag: Red, with green panel in the centre on which is a white crescent.

- Nearly half the population of the Maldives is under fifteen years old.
- Nowhere on any of the 1,200 islands in the Maldives does the ground rise higher than four metres above sea level.

Mali

Official name: Republic of Mali
History: Mali became a French colony at the end of the 19th century. In 1960 it became an independent republic.
World location: North-west Africa
Area: 1,240,000 km^2
Local time: GMT
Population: 8,920,000
Language: French is the official language; local languages, principally Bambara, are also spoken.
Religion: Moslem
Capital: Bamako
Other major centres: Ségou, Mopti, Sikasso
Money: CFA franc = 100 centimes
Weather: Hot and dry in the desert areas of the north and east, cooler and wetter in the south and west
Main rivers: Senegal, Niger, Faleme

Main mountain ranges: Mandingué Plateau, Adrar des Iforas
National day: 22 September
National flag: Three vertical stripes of green, yellow and red.

● Many of the people in Mali are nomads who have no fixed living place. They travel through the desert country living in tents made from camel hair.

Malta

Official name: Republic of Malta
History: Malta has been occupied by many nations since ancient times. The islands came under British protection in the 19th century. Malta became independent in 1964.
World location: Mediterranean Sea. The islands that make up Malta lie about halfway between Gibraltar at the western end of the Mediterranean and the Egyptian port of Port Said at the eastern end.
Area: 316 km^2
Local time: 1 hour ahead of GMT (summer time 2 hours ahead)
Population: 340,000
Language: Maltese and English are the official languages
Religion: Christian (Roman Catholic)
Capital: Valletta
Money: Maltese lira = 100 cent
Weather: Hot, dry summers and mild winters. Most of the rain falls between October and March.
National day: 31 March
National flag: Two vertical stripes of white and red. In

Malta

1942 King George VI awarded Malta the British medal known as the George Cross, and this is represented on the Maltese flag in the upper corner next to the flagpole.

- According to local tradition St Paul was shipwrecked near Malta in AD 60 and converted the people to Christianity.
- Malta has some of the oldest surviving buildings in Europe, which date from the third and fourth centuries BC.
- Maltese is the only Arabic language that is written in the Roman alphabet, the alphabet in which English and other European languages are written.

Martinique

Official name: Department of Martinique
History: Martinique has been a French colony for most of its history since the 17th century.
World location: Eastern Caribbean Sea. Martinique is one of the Windward Islands.
Area: 1,102 km²
Local time: 4 hours behind GMT
Population: 330,000
Language: French is the official language; Creole is also spoken.
Religion: Christian (Roman Catholic)
Capital: Fort-de-France
Money: Franc = 100 centimes
Weather: Warm and comfortable, coolest from December to May

- The first wife of Napoleon Bonaparte, the Empress Josephine, was born on the island of Martinique.

● Martinique is a mountainous volcanic island. Its highest volcano is Mont Peleé (1,351 metres), which erupted in 1902 and destroyed the town of St Pierre, killing 40,000. According to some reports the only survivor was a prisoner in the town's gaol.

Mauritania

Official name: Islamic Republic of Mauritania
History: Mauritania formed part of French West Africa at the beginning of this century. In 1960 the country became fully independent.
World location: North-west Africa, with its western coastline on the Atlantic Ocean
Area: 1,030,700 km²
Local time: GMT
Population: 1,920,000
Language: Arabic and French are the official languages.
Religion: Moslem
Capital: Nouakchott
Other major centres: Nouadhibou, Kaédi, Zouérate
Money: Ouguiya = 5 khoums
Weather: Hot and dry, with sea breezes on the coast
Main river: Senegal
National day: 28 November
National flag: Green, with a yellow crescent beneath a yellow star in the centre.

● Half of Mauritania is covered with sand dunes.
● Four-fifths of the country's population are nomads.
● Mauritania is the second least densely populated country in the world. There are 1.8 people to every square kilometre in Mauritania. If the UK was as sparsely

populated its population would be less than 440,000, or about 7.75 per cent of its actual population.

Mauritius

History: The sailors of several different nations from both Asia and Europe have visited Mauritius during its history. The British took control of the island in 1810. Mauritius became independent in 1968.

World location: Western Indian Ocean. Mauritius is the main one of a group of islands 900 km east of Madagascar.

Area: 2,040 km²

Local time: 4 hours ahead of GMT

Population: 1,110,000

Language: English

Religion: Mainly Hindu; smaller communities of Christians and Moslems

Capital: Port Louis

Other major centres: Beau Bassin-Ross Hill, Curepipe. Quatre Bornes

Money: Mauritius rupee = 100 cents

Weather: Humid most of the year. Most rain falls in the summer.

National day: 12 March

National flag: Four horizontal stripes of red, blue, yellow and green.

- The *sega* is a popular form of entertainment on Mauritius, both dance and song. Performers often change the words of the song to make it more up-to-date.
- At Christian baptisms on Mauritius little bags of *dragees* (grains of crunchy sugar icing) are given out.

● Before the arrival of European sailors Mauritius was the home of the large flightless bird — the dodo. Since it could not fly and was rather clumsy on the ground, the dodo was easy to catch and within a couple of centuries had been hunted to extinction, giving us the expression 'dead as a dodo'.

Mexico

Official name: United States of Mexico
History: Before the 16th century Mexico consisted of a number of Indian empires. Spain occupied the country from the 16th to the 18th centuries. Mexico became independent in 1821.
World location: North America, with its western coastline on the Pacific Ocean and eastern coastline on the Gulf of Mexico
Area: 1,958,201 km^2
Local time: From 6 hours behind GMT to 8 hours behind GMT. In summer these times are 1 hour less.
Population: 82,730,000
Language: Spanish
Religion: Christian (Roman Catholic)
Capital: Mexico City
Other major centres: Guadalajara, Monterrey, Puebla de Zaragoza, Léon de los Aldamas, Cuidad Juárez, Cuidad Rosales
Money: Mexican peso = 100 centavos
Weather: The north is dry with wide variations in temperature. The south is humid and tropical. The central plateau is cooler and less humid.
Main rivers: Rio Grande, Balsas, Grijalva
Main mountain ranges: Sierra Madre Occidental, Sierra Madre Oreintal, Sierra Madre de Sur

Mexico

National day: 16 September
National flag: Three vertical stripes of green, white and red. In the centre of the white stripe is the emblem of Mexico, an eagle standing on a cactus plant with a snake in its beak. This emblem represents an ancient legend from the time of the Aztec Indians. According to the legend the Aztecs were told to build their capital where they saw an eagle standing on a cactus plant. When they did see this they obeyed the legend and began to build on what is the site of Mexico City today.

- Today Mexico City is the fastest-growing city on earth. According to the United Nations prediction the population of Mexico City will have almost doubled by the end of this century to reach a total of 31,616,000 people – slightly more than the present population living in the whole of Argentina!
- The Gulf of Mexico is the largest gulf in the world.
- The world's smallest breed of dog, the Chihuahua, originally came from Mexico.
- At Christmas, Mexican children play the *pinata* game which is rather like Blindman's Bluff. The *pinata* itself is a container made of clay or papier mâché, often shaped like an animal, and filled with sweets or toys. The aim of the game is to smash the *pinata* with a stick while blindfolded.
- *Jai alai* is a popular Mexican sport that calls for quick reactions and a quick eye. Players throw a ball against a wall and catch it using a racket shaped like a long basket. This helps give the ball tremendous speed, making *jai alai* the fastest ball game in the world. *Jai alai* balls have been known to travel at 302 km/hr.
- In Mexican cooking the *tortilla* is as well known as pasta in Italian cooking. *Tortillas* are thin pancakes made of corn which can be eaten plain or rolled up with a spicy filling. An unusual fruit eaten in Mexico is the prickly pear, which is a sort of cactus. The fruit and leaves have

to be cooked first, but once they are prepared they taste delicious.

Monaco

Official name: Principality of Monaco
History: From the 13th century the tiny principality of Monaco has belonged to the Grimaldi family.
World location: Southern Europe. Monaco is completely surrounded by France except for its coastline on the Mediterranean Sea.
Area: 1.9 km²
Local time: 1 hour ahead of GMT (summer time 2 hours ahead)
Population: 30,000
Language: French
Religion: Christian (Roman Catholic)
Money: Franc = 100 centimes
Weather: Warm summers and mild winters
Main river: Vesubie
National day: 19 November
National flag: Two horizontal stripes of red and white.

- The coastline of Monaco stretches for 5.61 km, making it the shortest national coastline in the world.
- Monaco is the most densely populated country in Europe, with nearly 15,800 to the square kilometre.

Mongolia

Official name: Mongolian People's Republic
History: Mongolia has been controlled by both Russia and China since the end of the 17th century. In 1921 it became an independent republic.
World location: Central Asia
Area: 1,565,000 km²
Local time: 8 hours ahead of GMT (summer time 9 hours ahead)
Population: 2,090,000
Language: Mongolian
Religion: Mainly Buddhist
Capital: Ulan Bator
Other major centres: Darkhan, Erdenet
Money: Tugrik = 100 mongo
Weather: Dry, with very cold winters and mild summers
Main rivers: Selenge/ Orhon, Hereleng
Main mountain ranges: Altai Mountains, Hangayn Nuruu
National day: 11 July
National flag: Three vertical stripes of red, blue and red. On the red stripe next to the flagpole is a golden star and under it an ancient religious symbol, a *soyonbo*, also in gold.

- Mongolia is the least densely populated country on earth with just 1.3 people to every square kilometre.
- In the Middle Ages the great Mongol empire ruled over by Genghis Khan and Kublai Khan stretched right across Asia from China in the east to Turkey in the west and as far south as India.
- For centuries the nomads of Mongolia have lived in portable huts called *ger* or *yurt*. These are constructed of layers of felt which make very good insulation and help

protect the people living inside from the intense heat and cold.

Montserrat

Official name: Colony of Montserrat
History: Montserrat has been a British colony since the 17th century.
World location: Eastern Caribbean Sea
Area: 102 km^2
Local time: 4 hours behind GMT
Population: 10,000
Language: English
Religion: Christian
Capital: Plymouth
Money: East Caribbean dollar = 100 cents
Weather: Tropical; hottest from June to November
National flag: The flag of Montserrat is the British Blue Ensign with the island's shield on a white disc.

- Christopher Columbus named Montserrat after a mountain in Spain.
- The island is world famous for the soft Sea Island cotton which is grown on small farms all over Montserrat.
- Montserrat has been called 'the Emerald Isle' because of the great number of settlers from the original 'emerald isle' of Ireland, who came to Montserrat in the 17th century.

Morocco

Official name: Kingdom of Morocco
History: In 1956 the independent Kingdom of Morocco was created from French and Spanish territories and the international zone of Tangier.
World location: North-west Africa, with its western coastline on the Atlantic Ocean and northern coastline on the Mediterranean Sea
Area: 458,730 km^2
Local time: GMT
Population: 23,910,000
Language: Arabic, Berber; French and Spanish are also spoken.
Religion: Mainly Moslem
Capital: Rabat
Other major centres: Casablanca, Fez, Marrakesh, Meknes
Money: Dirham = 100 centimes
Weather: Very hot in the desert regions of the south, cooler in the mountains, warm and sunny on the coast
Main rivers: Oued Dra, Oued Oum-er-Rbia
Main mountain ranges: Haut (Grand) Atlas, Moyen (Middle Atlas), Anti Atlas
National day: 3 March
National flag: Red, with a green star made from interlaced lines in the centre.

- In Arabic Morocco means 'The Farthest West'.
- The University of Karueein was established in Fez in the year 859. It is the oldest existing educational institution in the world.

Mozambique

Official name: People's Republic of Mozambique
History: Mozambique was a Portuguese colony from the 16th century until the country became independent in 1975.
World location: South-east Africa, with its eastern coastline on the Indian Ocean
Area: 799,380 km^2
Local time: 2 hours ahead of GMT
Population: 14,930,000
Language: Portuguese is the official language; Swahili is also spoken.
Religion: The largest religious group follows traditional local religions. There are smaller numbers of Christians and Moslems.
Capital: Maputo
Other major centres: Beira, Nampula
Money: Mozambique metical = 100 centavos
Weather: Tropical and humid. The dry season lasts from June to September.
Main rivers: Limpopo, Zambezi, Rovuma
Main mountain range: Lebombo Range
National day: 25 June
National flag: Three horizontal stripes of green, black and yellow, with narrow white stripes above and below the black. On the side next to the flagpole is a red triangle containing a yellow star on which is an open white book and a rifle crossed with a hoe.

- One-fifth of Mozambique is covered by forests.
- Almost half the country's earnings come from selling shrimps, and the annual prawn catch amounts to over 5,500 tonnes.

Namibia

History: Namibia came under German protection in the 19th century. In 1915 South Africa took control of the country. In 1989 elections were held to form an independent government.

World location: South-west Africa, with its western coastline on the Atlantic Ocean

Area: 824,269 km^2

Local Time: 2 hours ahead of GMT

Population: 1,760,000

Language: Afrikaans; local languages are also spoken.

Religion: Christian (mainly Lutheran)

Capital: Windhoek

Money: South African rand = 100 cents

Weather: Dry and arid along the coast and in the Kalahari in the north and east, cooler on the higher plateau

Main rivers: Kunene River, Okavango, Zambesi, Orange

● The Kalahari Desert which covers part of Namibia actually receives 200 – 450 mm of rain a year. The land always appears to be bone dry because the water seeps into the ground very quickly. But deep wells can be dug to provide water.

Nauru

Official name: Republic of Nauru
History: From the 19th century until the First World War Nauru was controlled by Germany. Australia captured the island in 1914 and in 1968 Nauru became independent.
World location: West Pacific Ocean, 2,000 km north-east of Australia
Area: 21 km²
Local time: 12 hours ahead of GMT
Population: 8,100
Language: Nauruan and English
Religion: Christian
Money: Australian dollar = 100 cents
Weather: Tropical; sea breezes keep the temperature comfortable
National day: 31 January
National flag: Blue, with a narrow horizontal gold stripe across the centre representing the equator. Below the gold stripe and near the flagpole is a twelve-pointed gold star.

- Rainfall is low in Nauru and people have to be careful when they use it. Drinking water is collected in storage tanks on the roofs of houses, and in periods of drought water has to be imported from other countries and pumped ashore from ships.
- A large part of Nauru is made of a rich deposit of phosphates which are mined to be used as fertilizers. This has been the island's main source of income for most of this century, although all the phosphates will probably be extracted by the mid-1990s.

Nepal

Official name: Kingdom of Nepal

History: Nepal was unified as a single country in the 18th century by the king whose family still reigns.

World location: Central Asia. Nepal lies in the central Himalayas between Tibet and India.

Area: 147,181 km²

Local time: 5¾ hours ahead of GMT

Population: 18,230,000

Language: Nepali; Bihari is also spoken

Religion: Mainly Hindu

Capital: Kathmandu

Other major centres: Patan, Morang, Bhadgaon

Money: Nepalese rupee = 100 pice

Weather: Lower areas are humid and warm. The mountains are very cold in winter with heavy snowfalls.

Main rivers: Karnali, Naryani, Kosi

Main mountain range: Himalayas

National day: 28 December

National flag: Two right-angled triangles, one above the other. Both triangles are red and edged with blue. On the upper one is a white emblem for the moon, on the lower one a white emblem for the sun.

- Nepal is the world's only Hindu kingdom.
- The Himalayas, the world's highest range of mountains, cover nine-tenths of Nepal.
- The mountains are so remote and inaccessible that there are still reports that the *yeti* or 'abominable snowman' lives there. Several people claim to have seen it and expeditions have set out to find this mysterious creature, but so far no one has actually found a *yeti*.

- It was only forty years ago that visitors from western countries were first allowed to visit Nepal.
- At one time the Kathmandu valley was divided into three separate principalities which were only a few kilometres apart.
- On the southern slopes of the Himalayas in the northern areas of the country the Nepalese grow a wide range of herbs that are used to make medicines all over the world.

Netherlands

Official name: Kingdom of the Netherlands
History: The Netherlands became united as a kingdom in 1815. Germany occupied the country during the Second World War.
World location: Western Europe, with its western coastline on the North Sea
Area: 41,863 km²
Local time: 1 hour ahead of GMT (summer time 2 hours ahead)
Population: 14,760,000
Language: Dutch
Religion: Christian
Capital: The Hague
Other major centres: Rotterdam, Amsterdam, Utrecht, Eindhoven, Arnhem
Money: Guilder = 100 cents
Weather: Cool summers and mild winters
Main rivers: Maas (Meuse), Waal, Rhine, Ijssel
National flag: Three horizontal stripes of red, white and blue.

- There is an old Dutch saying that 'God created the

world, but the Dutch created Holland', which is based on the fact that over two-fifths of the land in the Netherlands has been reclaimed from the sea. The Netherlands were once called the Low Countries and much of the land is below sea level. However, by building defences against the sea and draining the *polders* (the land behind them), the Dutch have created some of their best farming land over a period of several hundred years.

- Christmas celebrations in the Netherlands begin earlier than they do in Britain. On 5 December, St Nicholas's Eve, a man dressed like a bishop, to represent the saint, arrives by ship in Amsterdam and is met by cheering crowds. St Nicholas is the patron saint of children and on St Nicholas's Eve he visits every house leaving presents for the children and taking the straw and carrots they leave for his horse. The Santa Claus who visits British homes on Christmas Eve is the same saint, his name a British variant of his Dutch name.

- The Netherlands is famous for its cheeses, including Edam and Gouda. The town of Hoorn has one market where nothing but cheese is sold. One dish from Indonesia (which once belonged to the Netherlands), has become very popular. This is called *rijsttafel*, and is an enormous meal made up of rice surrounded by about twenty-five different dishes containing eggs, seafood, vegetables and meat.

- As well as giving the English language Santa Claus, Dutch has given us many other words such as brandy, skate and yacht.

- One of the world's most valuable paintings, *Irises*, by the Dutch painter Vincent van Gogh, was sold for over £30,000,000, making it worth more than £4,500 per square centimetre.

- The microscope was invented in the Netherlands in 1590 by Zacharias Jenssen.

Netherlands Antilles

History: The Netherlands Antilles have been controlled by the Dutch since the 17th century.
World location: Two groups of islands, one 100 km north of the Venezuelan coast of South America, the other 800 km to the north-east
Area: 800 km^2
Local time: 4 hours behind GMT
Population: 190,000
Language: Dutch is the official language; Papiamento and English are also spoken.
Religion: Christian (mainly Roman Catholic)
Capital: Willemstad
Money: Netherlands Antillean Guilder = 100 cents
Weather: Tropical, with little temperature change throughout the year
National flag: White, with a vertical red stripe and a horizontal blue stripe. The blue stripe has five white stars.

- The island of Curacao has one of the largest ship-repair dry docks in the western world.

New Caledonia

Official name: Territory of New Caledonia
History: New Caledonia came under French control in the 19th century
World location: South-west Pacific Ocean. The territory consists of a group of islands about 1,200 km east of the coast of Queensland in north-eastern Australia
Area: 19,058 km^2

New Caledonia

Local time: 11 hours ahead of GMT
Population: 160,000
Language: French; local languages are also spoken
Religion: Mainly Christian
Capital: Noumea
Money: CFP franc = 100 centimes
Weather: Tropical, warm and humid. Heaviest rainfall February to May.

- Captain Cook gave New Caledonia its name because the islands reminded him of the Highlands of Scotland. Caledonia was the name the ancient Romans gave to Scotland.
- These islands are the home of the bulkiest starfish in the world, one specimen of which weighed 6 kg. Starfish are able to grow back arms and other parts of their body that they lose.
- The flightless *cagou* is the national bird of New Caledonia. It only hatches one egg a year.

New Zealand

Official name: Dominion of New Zealand
History: New Zealand became a British colony in the 19th century and gained its independence in 1907.
World location: South-west Pacific Ocean
Area: 268,046 km²
Local time: 13 hours ahead of GMT (from October to March 12 hours ahead)
Population: 3,290,000
Language: English
Religion: Christian
Capital: Wellington

Other major centres: Auckland, Christchurch, Hamilton, Dunedin
Money: New Zealand dollar = 100 cents
Weather: Mild winters, except in the far south which is colder; warm summers
Main rivers: Waikato, Clutha, Waihou, Rangitaiki
Main mountain range: Southern Alps
National day: 6 February
National flag: Blue, with the Union Jack in the upper corner next to the flagpole. Four red stars edged with white represent the Southern Cross, the same group of stars that appear on the Australian flag. The Southern Cross can only be seen from south of the equator.

- The people of New Zealand eat more butter and meat per head than anyone else in the world.
- The New Zealand tuatara is the only survivor of a group of reptiles that were living 170,000,000 years ago. It has the lowest body temperature of any living reptile (11°C) and has been known to go without breathing for sixty minutes.
- New Zealand became the first country to give women the right to vote in national elections when the law was passed in 1893.
- The average earnings in New Zealand are higher than in any other country in the world exept the USA and Canada. About seven out of ten New Zealand families own their own homes.
- Wellington is the most southerly capital in the world.
- Sheep farming is very important in New Zealand and the country has more than twenty sheep to every human inhabitant.
- At one time half of New Zealand was forested. Today forests cover only one-sixth of the country.
- Since New Zealand is such a long way from any other landmass it has developed plants that are found nowhere else in the world. Among these are tree ferns

that grow to a height of 15 metres. There were originally no native mammals in New Zealand except for bats, so flightless birds like the Kiwi were able to survive. However, the introduction of mammals such as rabbits, stoats, cats and deer has altered the country's natural balance.

- The kiwi, New Zealand's national emblem, lays a larger egg in proportion to the size of its body than any other bird.

Nicaragua

Official name: Republic of Nicaragua
History: Nicaragua was a Spanish colony until it became fully independent in 1838.
World location: Central America, with its western coastline on the Pacific and eastern coastline on the Caribbean Sea
Area: 127,849 km²
Local time: 6 hours behind GMT
Population: 3,620,000
Language: Spanish
Religion: Christian (mainly Roman Catholic)
Capital: Managua
Other major centres: Leon, Granada, Masaya, Chinandega
Money: Cordoba = 100 centavos
Weather: Hot and humid, with a wet season from May to January
Main rivers: Coco, Rio Grande, Escondido
Main mountain ranges: Cordillera Isabelia, Cordiullera de Darien
National day: 15 September
National flag: Three horizontal stripes of blue, white

and blue. In the centre of the white stripe is the
Nicaraguan coat of arms.

- Nicaragua is the largest in area of the republics of
  Central America, but also the least densely populated.
- Lake Nicaragua is also the largest lake in Central
  America.
- Almost half the land in Nicaragua is covered by forests.

Niger

Official name: Republic of Niger
History: Niger became a French territory in the 19th
century and remained under French control until 1960
when the country gained its independence.
World location: North central Africa
Area: 1,267,000 km²
Local time: 1 hour ahead of GMT
Population: 6,690,000
Language: French is the official language; Hausa is also
spoken.
Religion: Moslem
Capital: Niamey
Other major centres: Zinder, Maradi, Tahoua
Money: CFA franc = 100 centimes
Weather: Hot and dry, with little rain in the desert areas
of the north
Main rivers: Niger, Dillia
Main mountain ranges: Aïr, Plateau du Djado
National day: 18 December
National flag: Three horizontal stripes of orange, white
and green with an orange disc in the middle of the white
stripe.

153

Niger

- Only about eighty people in every 1,000 in Niger can read and write.
- Between September and March it is possible for sea-going ships to sail up the Niger to Niamey, 300 km inside Niger.

Nigeria

Official name: Federal Republic of Nigeria
History: Nigeria was unified under British protection in 1914. The country became independent in 1960.
World location: West Africa, with its southern coastline on the Atlantic Ocean
Area: 923,768 km^2
Local time: 1 hour ahead of GMT
Population: 105,470,000
Language: English; local languages like Hausa and Ibo are also spoken
Religion: Moslem and Christian
Capital: Lagos. A new federal capital is being completed at Abuja.
Other major centres: Ibadan, Ogbomosho, Kano, Oshogobo, Ilorin, Abeokuta
Money: Naira = 100 kobo
Weather: Hot and humid on the coast, drier inland
Main rivers: Niger, Benue, Cross
Main mountain range: Jos Plateau
National day: 1 October
National flag: Three vertical stripes of green, white, green.

- There are more than 250 ethnic groups in Nigeria.
- Much of Nigeria's literature is spoken rather than being

written down, and takes the form of chants, folk stories and riddles.

- Some of the oldest remains of human settlement have been found in Nigeria. Stone tools and rock paintings have been discovered that date back 40,000 years.
- The principal foods in Nigeria include beans, corn, rice and yams. Nigerian food is often cooked in peanut oil and uses lots of red peppers. Most Nigerians eat little meat.

Norfolk Island

History: Captain Cook discovered Norfolk Island in the 18th century and until the middle of the 19th century it was an island prison. At the end of the 19th century Australia took control of the island.

World location: South-west Pacific Ocean, 1,500 km north-east of Sydney, Australia

Area: 36 km^2

Local time: 11½ hours ahead of GMT

Population: 2,000

Language: English

Religion: Christian

Money: Australian dollar = 100 cents

Weather: Sub-tropical, warm all year.

- Tourism is very important to the economy of Norfolk Island. Norfolk Islanders pay no income tax on money they earn on the island, although the island's 'government' earns money from the sale of postage stamps and local taxes on goods bought and sold.

Norway

Official name: Kingdom of Norway
History: From the 15th century to the 19th century Norway was united with Denmark. For most of the 19th century it was united with Sweden and only became fully independent in 1905.
World location: North-west Europe, with its long coastline on the North Sea, the Atlantic Ocean and the Arctic Ocean
Area: 323,878 km^2
Local time: 1 hour ahead of GMT (summer time 2 hours ahead)
Population: 4,200,000
Language: Norwegian
Religion: Christian (mainly Lutheran)
Capital: Oslo
Other major centres: Bergen, Trondheim, Stavanger, Kristiansand
Money: Norwegian krone = 100 ore
Weather: Mild and wet along the west coast, colder inland and in the north
Main rivers: Glomma, Lagen, Tanaelv
Main mountain range: Langfjellene
National day: 17 May
National flag: Red, with white-edged blue cross.

- Norwegians have been travelling about on skis in winter for thousands of years. Skiing is the country's national sport and most Norwegians learn to ski before they go to school.
- Thanks to its mountains and steep-sided fjords, Norway generates more electricity by water power (hydro-electricity) than any other country in the world.

- The Viking sailors who set sail from Norway over several hundred years from the 8th century, travelled as far away as North America and Turkey. Viking sailors attacked Constantinople (now called Istanbul) and gave Russia its name; they called the people living in Russia the *Rus*.
- Sandwiches are very popular in Norway. They are often eaten at lunchtime and as an evening meal. Goat's cheese is a popular sandwich filler.
- If you've ever wondered where Hell is, look no further than Norway, where there's a town called Hell!

Oman

Official name: Sultanate of Oman
History: Portugal controlled Oman from the 16th century until the middle of the 17th century, when the present ruling family became sultans and took control.
World location: Middle East, with its south-east coastline on the Arabian Sea
Area: 212,457 km²
Local time: 4 hours ahead of GMT
Population: 1,380,000
Language: Arabic
Religion: Moslem
Capital: Muscat
Money: Omani rial = 1,000 baizas
Weather: Hot and humid desert climate
Main mountain range: Jabal Akhdas
National day: 18 November
National flag: Red, with a white panel on the upper side opposite the flagpole and a green panel on the lower side opposite the flagpole. In the corner nearest the flagpole is the national emblem of Oman in white.

Oman

- Oman is the oldest independent Arab country in the world.
- Oman has the tallest lampposts in the world. There are four which stand 63.5 metres high.
- This is one of the hottest countries in the world, where temperatures can reach 54°C.

Pakistan

Official name: Islamic Republic of Pakistan
History: Pakistan was created in 1947 out of a number of territories that had belonged to British India. Orginally it was divided into East and West Pakistan, but East Pakistan became independent and was renamed Bangladesh in 1971.
World location: South-west Asia, with its southern coastline on the Arabian Sea
Area: 796,095 km²
Local time: 5 hours ahead of GMT
Population: 105,410,000
Language: Urdu, Punjabi; English and other local languages are also spoken.
Religion: Moslem
Capital: Islamabad
Other major centres: Karachi, Lahore, Faisalabad, Rawalpindi, Hyderabad, Multan
Money: Pakistan rupee = 100 paisa
Weather: Hot and dry over most of the country. The mountains of the north are very cold in winter with heavy snowfalls
Main rivers: Indus and tributaries
Main mountain ranges: Hindu Kush, Pamirs, Karakorum
National day: 23 March, 14 August

National flag: Green, with a white vertical stripe next to the flagpole. On the green part are a white crescent moon and a white star.

- Four thousand years ago a great civilization flourished in the Indus valley in what is now Pakistan. In one of its cities, Mohenjo-daro, most of the houses were built with drains and lavatories.
- Fewer people live in Baluchistan, the province in the south-west of Pakistan which occupies more than a quarter of the country's total area, than live in the port city Karachi.
- In 1985 just under three-quarters of the people in Pakistan were unable to read and write.
- Just under half the children aged between five and nine go to school in Pakistan, although primary education is free and compulsory.

Panama

Official name: Republic of Panama
History: Panama was part of Colombia until it became independent in 1903.
World location: Central America. Panama is at the sourthern end of Central America. Since the country runs from east to west, the Caribbean Sea is to the north and the Pacific Ocean to the south.
Area: 77,046 km^2
Local time: 5 hours behind GMT
Population: 2,320,000
Language: Spanish
Religion: Christian (mainly Roman Catholic)
Capital: Panama City
Other major centres: Colón, David

Panama

Money: Balboa = 100 centesimos
Weather: Hot and humid
Main rivers: Tuira/ Chuchnaque, Bayano, Santa Maria
Main mountain ranges: Serrania de Tabasara, Cordillera de San Blas
National day: 3 November
National flag: Four coloured squares: white in the upper corner next to the flagpole with a blue star, blue below it, white in the lower corner opposite the flagpole with a red star and a red square above that.

- The Panama Canal, which cuts through the country, is one of the busiest waterways in the world and the only canal in the world that links two oceans (the Atlantic and the Pacific). However, sailing from the Atalantic to the Pacific is not just a simple matter of sailing east to west. Because of the way in which the canal is constructed, the Atlantic entrance is actually further west than the Pacific entrance.
- Panama hats, which are obviously named after Panama, did not originate in the country. They were first made in Ecuador. The mistake over the name dated from the 17th century when Panama became the centre for shipping the hats to other countries.
- The most popular sport in Panama is baseball, which was brought by American construction workers when they came to dig the canal in the 19th century.
- Panamanian cooking has an unusual and tasty way of preparing fish in a recipe called *corvina al horna*, in which the fish is baked in coconut milk.

Papua New Guinea

Official name: Independent State of Papua New Guinea

History: Papua came under Australian protection in the 19th century. The German colony in New Guinea was added to it after the First World War. Papua New Guinea became fully independent in 1975.

World location: West Pacific Ocean. Papua New Guinea consists of the eastern part of the island of New Guinea and several hundred nearby islands.

Area: 462,840 km²

Local time: 10 hours ahead of GMT

Population: 3,560,000

Language: English, Pidgin; 700 local languages are also spoken.

Religion: Christian; traditional local religions are also followed.

Capital: Port Moresby

Other major centres: Lae, Rabaul, Madang

Money: Kina = 100 toea

Weather: Hot and humid all year

Main rivers: Fly, Strickland, Sepik

Main mountain range: Bismarck Range

National day: 16 September

National flag: The flag is divided diagonally into two triangles. The upper triangle is red with a gold bird of paradise. The lower one is black with five white stars representing the group of stars called the Southern Cross.

- Almost 30,000 species of orchid are found in Papua New Guinea.
- Schoolchildren in Papua New Guinea are taught practical farming and other basic skills which they can use in

their home villages, as well as the sort of subjects usually taught in school.

- This is the home of the longest lizard in the world, the huge Salvadori monitor lizard which can be 4.74 metres long.
- The world's largest moth, the Hercules moth, also lives in Papua New Guinea. This has a wingspan of 280 mm.
- Papua New Guinea is the home of the Tree Kangaroo, which spends most of its life living in the branches of trees.

Paraguay

Official name: Republic of Paraguay
History: Paraguay was a Spanish colony from the 16th century until it became independent in 1811.
World location: Central South America
Area: 406,752 km²
Local time: 3 hours behind GMT (from April to September 4 hours behind)
Population: 4,040,000
Language: Spanish; Guarani is also spoken
Religion: Christian (mainly Roman Catholic)
Capital: Asunción
Other major centres: Presidente Stroessner, Pedro Juan Caballero, Encarnacion
Money: Guarani = 100 centimos
Weather: Hot and humid, with a short dry season from July to September
Main rivers: Paraguay, Parana, Pilcomayo
Main mountain ranges: Cordillera Amambay, Sierra de Maracaju
National day: 14 May
National flag: Three horizontal stripes of red, white and

blue. On one face the white stripe has the arms of Paraguay, on the other face the white band has a lion and the inscription *Paz y Justicia*, 'Peace and Justice'. This is the only flag in the world to have two different faces.

- The name Paraguay comes from the Indian words meaning 'a decorated river'.
- Paraguay is the world's biggest producer of petitgrain oil, which is used to make marmalade and perfume.
- Between 1865 and 1870 Paraguay fought a terrible war against Argentina, Brazil and Uruguay in which more than half the country's people and most of its men were killed.
- As well as acting as the capital of Paraguay, Asunción is also the chief port in spite of lying almost 1,530 km from the sea.

Peru

Official name: Republic of Peru
History: Before the Spanish conquest in the 16th century Peru had been the centre of a powerful empire ruled by an Indian nation known as the Incas. For 300 years Peru was the most important Spanish territory in South America before it became fully independent in 1824.
World location: West of South America, with its western coastline on the Pacific Ocean
Area: 1,285,216 km^2
Local time: 5 hours behind GMT
Population: 21,260,000
Language: Spanish; Quechua is also spoken
Religion: Christian (Roman Catholic)

Peru

Capital: Lima
Other major centres: Arequipa, Chiclayo, Callao, Cuzco
Money: Inti = 100 soles
Weather: Dry in the southern desert, humid on the coast, cooler in the higher areas with snow all year round on the high mountains.
Main rivers: Amazon, Ucayali
Main mountain range: Andes
National day: 28 July
National flag: Three vertical stripes of red, white, red, with the country's coat of arms in the centre of the white stripe.

- The Incas developed hundreds of varieties of potato. They also invented a successful method of preserving potatoes, by freezing them. On cold nights the potatoes were left outside to freeze hard and were then stored. When they were needed for cooking, they had only to be left in the sun to thaw.

- One of the highest ransoms ever paid was that for the last Inca king Atahualpa, who was captured by the Spanish in 1533. His nation raised an estimated ransom of $170,000,000 in gold and silver.

- Peru has the world's deepest canyon, El Canon de Colca, which is 3,223 metres deep.

- The Nazca lines that can be seen by anyone flying over the Nazca plateau in the Peruvian desert are still one of the great mysteries of South America. Archaeologists believe that the lines were drawn in the dark earth over a period of 800 years from the beginning of the fifth century. Some of them are huge, stretching for a distance of nearly 65 km, and from the air they can be seen to show animals, flowers, insects, gods and geometric patterns. Who drew these lines and why they were drawn so that they could only be seen from the sky has never been adequately answered.

Philippines

Official name: Republic of Philippines
History: The Philippines were conquered by Spain in the 16th century. They passed to the USA at the end of the 19th century and became fully independent in 1946.
World location: Western Pacific Ocean. The Philippines consists of a chain of 7,000 islands, the largest of which are Luzon and Mindanao
Area: 300,000 km^2
Local time: 8 hours ahead of GMT
Population: 58,728,000
Language: Philipino; many local languages are also spoken
Religion: Christian (mainly Roman Catholic); smaller communities of Moslems and Aglipayans
Capital: Manila
Other major centres: Quezon City, Davao, Cebu, Caloocan, Makati, Zamboanga
Money: Philippine peso = 100 centavos
Weather: Hot and humid, except in the mountains
Main rivers: Cagayan, Pampanga, Abra
Main mountain ranges: Cordillera Central (on Luzon), Diuta Range (on Mindanao)
National day: 12 June
National flag: Two horizontal stripes of blue and red. Next to the flagpole is a white triangle with a gold sun and three gold stars.

- There are more Christians living in the Philippines than in any other country in Asia.
- The seas around the Philippines have produced the world's largest pearl, weighing 6.37 kg. This was found inside the shell of a giant clam.
- The world's largest sea cucumber lives in the waters

around the Philippines. Sea cucumbers are used to make bath loofahs.
- The yo-yo was developed in the Philippines, but not as a toy. The original yo-yos were weapons of war.

Pitcairn

Official name: Colony of the Pitcairn Islands
History: Pitcairn was first discovered in the 18th century, but it was thirty years before anyone went to live there. The first settlers were the mutineers from the ship HMS *Bounty*, who landed on the island with a group of companions from Tahiti. No one knew where they were until nearly twenty years later when the islands were again visited. In the middle of the 19th century the population had grown too large for the island and all the people were moved away to a larger one. A few years later forty-three of them went back to Pitcairn and their descendants have been there ever since.
World location: South central Pacific Ocean, four islands halfway across the Pacific between New Zealand and Panama.
Area: 5 km²
Local time: 9 hours behind GMT
Population: 57
Language: English
Religion: Christian
Money: New Zealand dollar = 100 cents
Weather: Warm and comfortable throughout the year
National flag: British Blue Ensign with the arms of Pitcairn.

● The island of Pitcairn was named after Robert Pitcairn, the crew member of the expedition who first sighted it in 1767.

Poland

Official name: Polish Republic
History: Poland was a powerful kingdom in the Middle Ages. The country was divided between Russia, Austria and Prussia during the 18th century. Poland becme independent again after the First World War in 1918. Germany and the USSR invaded the country in 1939. By 1945 the USSR controlled the whole of the country and a communist republic was created. In 1989 a new government was formed by the free trade union Solidarity which had wide support among the Polish people.
World location: Eastern Europe
Area: 312,683 km^2
Local time: 1 hour ahead of GMT (summer time 2 hours ahead)
Population: 37,860,000
Language: Polish
Religion: Christian (Roman Catholic)
Capital: Warsaw
Other major centres: Lódz, Kraków, Wrocaw, Poznań, Gdańsk, Szczecin
Money: Zloty = 100 groszy
Weather: Short, wet summers and cold, snowy winters
Main rivers: Wisa (Vistula)/ Narew, Odra (Oder)
Main mountain ranges: Carpathian Mountains (Tatras), Beskids
National day: 22 July
National flag: Two horizontal bands of white and red.

- Poland is the world's second largest producer of potatoes and rye.
- In 1978 John Paul II became the first Polish pope. He was also the first pope from a Communist country and the first non-Italian pope since 1523.
- Polish Plain Spirit is the country's strongest vodka and at 98 percent proof the strongest drink in the world.
- Honey plays an important part in Polish cooking. Torun, the city where Copernicus (the astronomer who founded the modern study of the stars) was born, has been famous for its honey cakes since he was alive in the Middle Ages.

Portugal

Official name: Portuguese Republic
History: Portugal has been independent since the 12th century, except for one short period of Spanish occupation at the end of the 16th century.
World location: South-west Europe. Portugal shares the Iberian peninsula with Spain and has a western coastline on the Atlantic Ocean.
Area: 92,082 km²
Local time: GMT (summer time 1 hour ahead of GMT)
Population: 10,410,000
Language: Portuguese
Religion: Christian (Roman Catholic)
Capital: Lisbon
Other major centres: Porto, Amadora, Setubal, Coimbra
Money: Escudo = 100 centavos
Weather: Hot and very dry in the south, rainier winters in the inland areas, cooler and damper in the north

Main river: Rio Tejo (Tagus)
Main mountain range: Serra da Estrela
National day: 10 June
National flag: Two vertical stripes of green and red. The red stripe is twice the width of the green. The national coat of arms sits on the dividing line between the two colours.

- Bullfighting is as popular in Portugal as it is in Spain, but there is one important difference between the sport in the two countries. In Portugal the bulls are not killed.
- The town of Fatima has been a centre for Christian pilgrims ever since 1917 when three children from the town saw a vision of the Virgin Mary who spoke to them.
- The Portuguese Water Dog is a breed of dog that lives up to its name by being a good swimmer. The dog has webbed feet which help in the water. It is capable of swimming 8 km and of diving to depths of 3.7 metres. Portuguese fishermen have used the dogs for hundreds of years to pull nets and fish from the sea.
- Portugal is the world's leading producer of cork. Over 100,000 tonnes of cork are sent to other countries every year. The cork is actually the bark of the Cork Oak, which is cut off every ten years, soaked in water and pressed into flat sheets.

Puerto Rico

Official name: Commonwealth of Puerto Rico
History: Puerto Rico was a Spanish territory until it was passed to the control of the USA at the end of the 19th century.
World location: Caribbean Sea, 80 km east of the Dominican Republic

Puerto Rico

Area: 8,860 km²
Local time: 4 hours behind GMT
Population: 3,290,000
Language: Spanish and English
Religion: Christian (Roman Catholic)
Capital: San Juan
Other major centres: Bayamon, Ponce, Carolina
Money: US dollar = 100 cents
Weather: Sub-tropical; warm all year
Main mountain range: Cordillera Central

- Puerto Rico has over 370 people for every square kilometre, making it one of the most densely populated countries in the Americas.
- All women in Puerto Rico won the right to vote in elections in 1936.

Qatar

Official name: State of Qatar
History: Qatar was under British protection from 1916 until 1971, when it became independent.
World location: Middle East. Qatar occupies the Qatar peninsula on the west coast of the Persian Gulf and some offshore islands.
Area: 11,437 km²
Local time: 3 hours ahead of GMT
Population: 330,000
Language: Arabic
Religion: Moslem
Capital: Doha
Other major centres: Dukhan, Umm Said, Ruwais
Money: Qatar riyal = 100 dirhams
Weather: Hot and humid

National day: 3 September
National flag: Maroon, with white stripe next to the flagpole. The line between the two colours is jagged, like the teeth of a saw.

- Qatar is the richest country in the world if its annual income is divided among its citizens. National earnings per person in Qatar run at almost $23,000 a year.
- Qatar is also one of the very few countries in the world where no income tax is paid.
- Women are not allowed to drive in Qatar.

Romania

History: Romania was part of the Turkish Ottoman Empire until the end of the First World War. The country became independent in 1918. At the end of the Second World War it had been occupied by the USSR and a Communist republic was formed. In December 1989 the dictatorship of Nicolae Ceausescu was overthrown and a new government was sworn in after fighting in many parts of the country.
World location: Eastern Europe, with its eastern coastline on the Black Sea
Area: 237,500 km^2
Local time: 2 hours ahead of GMT (summer time 3 hours ahead)
Population: 23,050,000
Language: Romanian
Religion: Christian (mainly Romanian Orthodox)
Capital: Bucharest
Other major centres: Brasov, Constanta, Timisoara, Iasi, Cluj-Napoca
Money: Leu = 100 bani

Romania

Weather: Summers hot and humid, winters cold and snowy
Main rivers: Dunărea (Danube), Mureș, Prut
Main mountain range: Carpathian Mountains
National day: 23 August
National flag: Three vertical stripes of blue, yellow and red, with the national coat of arms in the middle of the yellow stripe.

- Romania means 'the land of the Romans' and the country was given this name because the people can trace their origins and language back to the ancient Romans who once settled here.
- Romania, or more accurately the region called Transylvania, is the legendary home of the vampire count of the famous novel and many horror films — Count Dracula.

Rwanda

Official name: Rwanda Republic
History: Rwanda was governed by Belgium for most of this century until it became independent in 1962.
World location: Central Africa
Area: 26,338 km²
Local time: 2 hours ahead of GMT
Population: 6,750,000
Language: Kinyarwanda and French are the official languages.
Religion: Christian (mainly Roman Catholic)
Capital: Kigali
Other major centres: Butare, Ruhengeri, Gisenyi
Money: Rwanda franc = 100 centimes

Weather: Hot and humid in lowlands, cooler in highlands
Main river: Luvironza (headwaters of the River Nile)
Main mountain range: Chaine des Mitumba
National day: 1 July
National flag: Three vertical stripes of red, yellow and green with the letter 'R' on the yellow stripe.

- There is roughly one telephone in Rwanda for every 873 people and one radio for every thirty-seven people.
- The mountainous area of western Rwanda is home to the Mountain gorilla, one of the two largest primates living on earth. The largest of these stand 172.5 cm high and weigh 155 kg.

St Christopher Nevis

Official name: State of St Christopher-Nevis
History: St Kitts-Nevis, as the island group is often known, became a British colony in the 17th century. The islands became fully independent in 1983.
World location: Eastern Caribbean Sea, one of the Leeward Islands
Area: 267 km^2
Local time: 4 hours behind GMT
Population: 50,000
Language: English
Religion: Christian
Capital: Basseterre
Other major centre: Charlestown
Money: East Caribbean dollar = 100 cents
Weather: Comfortable all through the year thanks to a cool breeze
National day: 19 September

St Christopher Nevis

National flag: Two triangles of green in the top corner next to the flagpole and red in the corner diagonally opposite. The triangles are divided by a thick black stripe edged with two narrow yellow stripes. Two white stars appear on the black stripe.

- St Kitts was the first island in the British West Indies to be colonized.

- The island of Nevis was first discovered by Christopher Columbus, who gave it its name. Seeing the white clouds on top of the mountains, he thought they looked like snow and named the island after the Spanish for 'the snows', *las nievas*.
- The islands were originally called *Liamuiga*, meaning 'fertile land'.
- The islands have a small railway system but this is used entirely to transport sugar cane. All other transport is by road and sea.
- Admiral Horatio Nelson married Frances Nisbet on the island of Nevis during his service in the West Indies.

St Helena

Official name: Colony of St Helena and dependencies
History: St Helena has been a British possession since the 17th century.
World location: South Atlantic Ocean, 2,000 km west of the coast of Angola in West Africa
Area: 122 km²
Local time: GMT
Population: 5,900
Language: English
Religion: Christian

Capital: Jamestown
Money: Pound = 100 pence
Weather: Mild all year
National flag: British Blue Ensign with the shield of St Helena.

- St Helena has become famous in history as the last home of the French emperor Napoleon Bonaparte. He was exiled to the island in 1815, after his defeat at the Battle of Waterloo, and spent six years living there until he died in 1821.

St Lucia

History: The French and British have both settled on St Lucia at different times since the 16th century. Britain finally gained control in the 19th century and St Lucia became independent in 1979.
World location: Eastern Caribbean Sea, one of the Windward Islands
Area: 616 km^2
Local time: 4 hours behind GMT
Population: 130,000
Language: English
Religion: Christian
Capital: Castries
Money: East Caribbean dollar = 100 cents
Weather: Warm and moist
National day: 22 February
National flag: Blue, with a black triangle edged in white, inside which is a smaller yellow triangle.

- St Lucia has one of the most spectacular tourist attractions in the Caribbean. These are the two volcanic cones, topped by forest, that rise sharply out of the sea and are known as the *Pitons*.

St Pierre and Miquelon

History: St Pierre and Miquelon are all that is left of the French territories in North America which once stretched from Canada to the Gulf of Mexico. The islands have been a French possession since the 17th century.
World location: North-east of North America. The eight islands of St Pierre and Miquelon lie off the coast of Newfoundland.
Area: 242 km^2
Local time: 3 hours behind GMT (summer time 2 hours behind)
Population: 6,000
Language: French
Religion: Christian (Roman Catholic)
Capital: St Pierre
Money: French franc = 100 centimes
Weather: Mild summers, with cold winters

● The islands are mostly barren rocks, which makes them unsuitable for conventional farming. The main 'farm' animals raised are foxes and mink which are bred for their fur.

St Vincent and the Grenadines

History: The island of St Vincent changed hands between the French and British several times until the British finally gained control in the 18th century. The islands became fully independent in 1979.

World location: East Caribbean Sea, part of the Windward Islands, south of St Lucia

Area: 389 km^2

Local time: 4 hours behind GMT

Population: 110,000

Language: English

Religion: Christian

Capital: Kingstown

Money: East Caribbean dollar = 100 cents

Weather: Warm and moist

National day: 27 October

National flag: Three vertical stripes of blue, yellow and green. The yellow stripe is twice the width of the others and on it are three green diamonds in the shape of a 'V'.

- St Vincent and the Grenadines have a close connection with the international computer industry. The islands are an important source of arrowroot, which is used extensively in the manufacture of computer paper.
- The hummingbirds found on the island have very rapid wing beats. These range from ten to eighty beats a second, depending on species.
- The first breadfruit tree in the West Indies was brought to St Vincent by Captain Bligh, the commander of the British ship *Bounty*, who was cast adrift with eighteen others after the rest of the crew mutinied in the Pacific. The original breadfruit tree is still growing and can be

seen in the botanical gardens in Kingstown. These are the oldest botanical gardens in the western world.

Samoa, American

History: The USA took control of American Samoa in 1900.
World location: South central Pacific Ocean. Six main islands 2,900 km north-east of New Zealand.
Area: 195 km²
Local time: 11 hours behind GMT
Population: 40,000
Language: Samoan; English
Religion: Christian
Capital: Pago Pago
Money: US dollar = 100 cents
Weather: Tropical, warm all year

● An important event in American Samoa is the catching of the *palolo* (coral worm) which takes place when the moon and the tide reach a particular stage in their cycles. The *palolo* is considered to be a great delicacy and many people call it the caviar of the Pacific.

San Marino

Official name: Republic of San Marino
History: San Marino was founded as a city-state early in the 4th century and has remained independent ever since.

World location: Central Italy. San Marino is completely surrounded by Italy.
Area: 61 km²
Local time: 1 hour ahead of GMT (summer time 2 hours ahead)
Population: 20,000
Language: Italian
Religion: Christian (Roman Catholic)
Money: San Marino Lira = 100 centesimos
Weather: Warm summers, damp winters
National day: 3 September
National flag: Two horizontal bands of white and blue, with the national coat of arms in the middle.

- San Marino is the oldest republic in the world.
- Its national anthem is just four lines long.

São Tomé E Príncipe

Official name: Democratic Republic of Sao Tomé and Príncipe.
History: A Portuguese colony from the 16th century, Sao Tomé e Príncipe became independent in 1975.
World location: West Africa. A group of islands 200 km from the coast of Gabon. The main islands are Sao Tomé and Príncipe.
Area: 964 km²
Local time: GMT
Population: 110,000
Language: Portuguese is the official language; a Bantu language called Fang is also spoken.
Religion: Christian (mainly Roman Catholic)
Capital: São Tomé
Money: Dobra = 100 centavos

Sao Tomé E Príncipe

Weather: Warm and humid
National day: 12 July
National flag: Three horizontal stripes of green, yellow and green. The yellow stripe is twice the width of the others and contains two black stars. Next to the flagpole is a red triangle.

- Fishing for tuna is one of the most important industries in São Tomé e Príncipe. Although it is much larger than the mackerel, the tuna belongs to the same family of fishes. Different methods are used to catch tuna, but one involves a maze of nets designed so that the fish swim into a central box net where they can be caught. Fishermen have discovered that if a tuna meets an obstacle it instinctively turns to the right so this net maze is designed to keep the tuna turning right until they swim into the middle.

Saudi Arabia

Official name: Kingdom of Saudi Arabia
History: Saudi Arabia became an independent kingdom in 1927.
World location: Middle East. Saudi Arabia occupies the main centre of the Arabian peninsula, with a western coastline on the Red Sea and a north-eastern coastline on the Persian Gulf.
Area: 2,200,000 km²
Local time: 3 hours ahead of GMT
Population: 14,020,000
Language: Arabic
Religion: Moslem
Capital: Riyadh
Other major centres: Jedda, Mecca, Taif and Medina

Money: Saudi Riyal = 100 hallalas
Weather: Very hot and dry. Most of the country is desert
Main mountain range: Tiha matash Sham
National flag: Green, the colour of the Moslem religion, on which is written in white Arabic script 'There is no God but Allah and Mohammed is his prophet.' Below this is a curved white sword.

- The King Khalid International Airport is one of the biggest in the world and cost £2,100,000,000,000 to build.
- Saudi Arabia exports more oil than any other country.
- The city of Mecca is the birthplace of the prophet Mohammed. It is the holiest city in Islam and Moslems from all over the world visit it every year as one of their holy duties.
- Saudi boys and girls attend separate schools. Before 1926 the country's only schools were religious buildings called *kuttabs*.
- Saudi Arabia is the world's twelfth largest country. It is so dry that desert covers the whole country and there is not a single river in the entire kingdom.
- In spite of being covered by sand, Saudi Arabia has to import sand from other countries for its building work! Desert sand is not suitable for use in the construction industry.

Senegal

Official name: Republic of Senegal
History: Senegal was a French territory from the 17th century until 1960 when it became independent.
World location: West Africa, with its western coastline on the Atlantic Ocean

Senegal

Area: 196,192 km^2
Local time: GMT
Population: 7,110,000
Language: French
Religion: Mainly Moslem
Capital: Dakar
Other major centres: Thiès, Kaolak, Saint-Louis
Money: CFA franc = 100 centimes
Weather: Hot, with a short wet season and a long dry one
Main rivers: Gambia, Casamance, Senegal
Main mountain range: Fouta Djalon
National day: 14 April
National flag: Three vertical stripes of green, yellow and red, with a green star in the middle of the yellow stripe.

- Senegal is Africa's most westerly country.
- Many of the Cyar fishing boats in Senegal are carved from a single tree trunk. Some of the biggest of these can hold up to six people.

Seychelles

Official name: Republic of the Seychelles
History: The islands that form the Seychelles were captured by the British from the French at the end of the 18th century. They became independent in 1976.
World location: Western Indian Ocean, north of Madagascar
Area: 453 km^2
Local time: 4 hours ahead of GMT
Population: 70,000
Language: Creole; English and French are also spoken

Religion: Christian (mainly Roman Catholic)
Capital: Victoria
Money: Seychelles rupee = 100 cents
Weather: Warm and comfortable. Cooler and less humid from June to November
National day: 5 June
National flag: Two horizontal areas of red and green divided by a wavy white line.

- Bird Island in the Seychelles is the home of over 1,000,000 sooty terns.
- More than 500 specieis of plants have been recorded in the Seychelles, at least eighty of which do not grow anywhere else in the world.
- Coconuts are the main crop grown for export in the Seychelles, and breadfruit is an important source of food for the islanders. However rice, which is the principal food, has to be imported.

Sierra Leone

Official name: The Republic of Sierra Leone
History: Sierra Leone was a British colony from the end of the 18th century until it became independent in 1961.
World location: West Africa, with its western coastline on the Atlantic Ocean
Area: 71,740 km^2
Local time: GMT
Population: 3,950,000
Language: English; several local languages are also spoken
Religion: The largest religious group follow traditional local religions; there are smaller groups of Moslems and Christians.

Sierra Leone

Capital: Freetown
Other major centres: Makeni, Kenema, Bo
Money: Leone = 100 cents
Weather: Hot, with a rainy season from April to November when humidity is high
Main rivers: Siwa, Jong, Rokel
Main mountain range: Loma
National day: 27 April
National flag: Three horizontal stripes of green, white and blue.

- The name Sierra Leone originated from the Portuguese words meaning 'Mountain of the Lion'.
- Diamonds are found in swamps and at the bottom of river beds in Sierra Leone, making the country one of the most important diamond producers in the world.
- Education in primary schools is free in Sierra Leone but not compulsory, although parents are strongly encouraged to send their children to school.

Singapore

Official name: Republic of Singapore
History: Singapore was a British colony from the early 19th century until 1965 when the island became fully independent.
World location: South-east Asia, at the southern end of the Malay peninsula
Area: 620 km²
Local time: 8 hours ahead of GMT
Population: 2,650,000
Language: Malay, Chinese, Tamil and English
Religion: Buddhist, Taoist, Moslem, Christian, Hindu
Money: Singapore dollar = 100 cents

Weather: Hot and humid throughout the year
National day: 9 August
National flag: Two horizontal stripes of red and white.
In the upper corner next to the flagpole are a white
crescent moon and five white stars. The stars represent
Justice, Democracy, Peace, Equality and Progress.

- The name Singapore means 'City of the Lion'.
- Singapore's wealth is centred on its port, which covers
  an area of almost one 100 km^2 making it one of the
  largest in the world.
- The Westin Stamford hotel in Singapore is seventy-three
  floors high, making it one of the world's tallest hotels.
- Singapore is the largest oil-refining centre in the whole
  of Asia.
- Orchids are one of Singapore's most valuable exports.

Solomon Islands

History: The Solomon Islands came under British
protection in the 19th century and gained full
independence in 1978.
World location: South-west Pacific Ocean. The
Solomons are a group of islands to the east of Papua
New Guinea.
Area: 27,556 km^2
Local time: 11 hours ahead of GMT
Population: 300,000
Language: English is the official language; many local
languages are also spoken.
Religion: Christian
Capital: Honiara
Money: Solomon Islands dollar = 100 cents

Solomon Islands

Weather: Warm season November to April, cooler for the rest of the year
National day: 7 July
National flag: Two triangles of blue and green, divided by a diagonal yellow line. In the blue area are five white stars.

- One quarter of the people in the Solomon Islands belong to co-operatives, a system in which every member receives an equal share of what the co-operative earns.

Somalia

Official name: Somali Democratic Republic
History: Present-day Somalia was formed from two territories controlled by the UK and Italy. In 1960 these were joined to form an independent country.
World location: North-east Africa, with its eastern coastline on the Indian Ocean.
Area: 637,657 km^2
Local time: 3 hours ahead of GMT
Population: 7,110,000
Language: Somali and Arabic; English and Italian are also spoken.
Religion: Moslem
Capital: Mogadishu
Other major centres: Hargeisa, Baidoa, Burao
Money: Somali Shilling = 100 cetesimi
Weather: Hot and dry with much of the country desert. Cooler on the coast.
Main mountain ranges: Guban
National day: 21 October
National flag: Light blue, with a white star in the centre.

- One of the great medical successes of recent years has been the eradication of the deadly disease smallpox. Somalia was the last country in the world to report a case of smallpox and that was in 1979.
- About one person in four in Mogadishu has no fixed home in the capital. These people are partly nomadic, coming and going as they choose. As a result only a fairly small number of the children in Somalia have a regular education.
- Four people out of five in Somalia depend on the rearing of livestock such as cattle, goats and camels for their living.
- Milk, especially camel's milk, is the main food eaten by the Somalis. Rice is the commonest vegetable and mutton the commonest meat. In the south of the country a popular dish is coffee beans roasted with butter and eaten with milk.

South Africa

Official name: Republic of South Africa
History: In 1910 the Union of South Africa was formed from four British colonies in Southern Africa. In 1961 South Africa became a republic.
World location: South Africa, with coastlines on the Atlantic Ocean in the west and Indian Ocean in the east
Area: 1,221,037 km²
Local time: 2 hours ahead of GMT
Population: 33,750,000
Language: Afrikaans, English and local African languages
Religion: Christian
Capital: Pretoria

South Africa

Other major centres: Johannesburg, Durban, Port
Elizabeth, Bloemfontein
Money: Rand = 100 cents
Weather: Cool summers, mild winters
Main rivers: Orange, Limpopo, Vaal
Main mountain range: Drakensberg
National day: 31 May
National flag: Three horizontal stripes of orange, white
and blue, with the Union Jack and the flags of the
Orange Free State and the Transvaal together in the
middle.

- South Africa produces more gold and diamonds than
  any other country. The world's largest diamond, the
  Cullinan Diamond, was found in South Africa in 1905.
  Before it was cut it was the size of a man's fist. Part of
  this is now in the British Royal Sceptre as the cut
  diamond known as The Star of Africa.
- Mining is important in South Africa and the country has
  the deepest mine in the world, a gold mine known as the
  Western Deep. This is nearly 3,800 metres deep and the
  temperature at the bottom is 55°C, which means that
  huge refrigeration units must be used to cool the air for
  the men working down there.
- There is a policy in South Africa called *apartheid* which
  is designed to keep the races apart from each other. As
  a result white children go to white-only schools, Indians
  go to Indian-only schools, Coloureds go to Coloured-
  only schools, and black children to go to schools for
  blacks only. There are one or two small private schools
  run on non-racial lines where children are allowed to mix
  freely.

Spain

Official name: The Kingdom of Spain
History: For most of its history Spain has been a monarchy.
World location: South-west Europe. Spain occupies the largest part of the Iberian peninsula, which it shares with Portugal.
Area: 504,782 km²
Local time: 1 hour ahead of GMT (summer time 2 hours ahead)
Population: 39,050,000
Language: Spanish (Castilian); Catalan, Galician and Basque are also spoken.
Religion: Christian (Roman Catholic)
Capital: Madrid
Other major centres: Barcelona, Valencia, Seville, Zaragoza, Malaga, Bilbao
Money: Peseta = 100 Centimos
Weather: North cool summers and wet winters; interior hot summer and cold winters; hot summers and mild winters in the south
Main rivers: Ebro, Duero (Douro), Tajo (Tagus), Guadiana
Main mountain ranges: Pyrenees, Sierra Nevada
National day: 12 October
National flag: Three horizontal stripes of red, yellow and red. The yellow stripe is twice the width of the red ones and carries the national coat of arms near the flagpole.

- The giant panda Chi-Lin who lives in the zoo in Madrid is one of the most valuable zoo animals in the world. Giant pandas are so rare, both in zoos and in the wild, that Chi-Lin has been valued at over £1,000,000.
- The northern Spanish city of Pamplona celebrates a

fiesta every year called the 'Running of the Bulls'. Bulls are released through the streets and men have to run ahead of them to the bullring, where they can take part in amateur bullfights.

- A Spaniard named Jesus de Frotos has been awake for longer than anyone else over the last thirty-five years. He suffers from almost total insomnia (an inability to sleep), with the result that since 1954 he has only been able to doze and never to fall fully asleep.

- Most of the languages spoken in Europe share a number of common features, and language experts agree that they probably developed from a single ancient language which is known as Indo-European. However, the Basque language which is spoken in the Pyrenees of Spain and France seems to be an exception. Basque has no similiarities with other European languages and experts are still puzzled as to how it developed, or where it originated.

- Between the fifth and the thirteenth centuries most of Spain was ruled by an Arab nation from North Africa called the Moors. The religion of the country was Islam and many of the buildings still standing from that time look like buildings commonly seen in the Arab countries of the Middle East. Spanish music still has traces of middle eastern music today.

- The Romans occupied Spain several centuries before the Moors. Many of the things they built have lasted 2,000 years, one of which is the aqueduct in Segovia which used to bring water to the city from a spring sixteen kilometers away.

- Spanish cooking is growing in popularity as more and more people visit Spain. One dish that is a national favourite is a type of fish stew called *paella*, made from shrimp, lobster, chicken and vegetables, eaten with a flavoured rice. In warm weather a cold soup called *gazpacho* is popular. This consists of tomatoes, olive oil and spices.

Sri Lanka

Official name: Democratic Socialist Republic of Sri Lanka

History: From the 6th century BC until the 19th century Sri Lanka was a monarchy. The island then became a British colony until 1947 when it was granted independence.

World location: South Asia. The island of Sri Lanka is off the South-east coast of India.

Area: 65,610 km²

Local time: 5½ hours ahead of GMT

Population: 16,590,000

Language: Sinhala, English and Tamil

Religion: Mainly Buddhism; smaller numbers of Hindus, Christians and Moslems

Capital: Colombo

Other major centres: Dehiwela-Mt Lavinia, Moratuwa, Jaffna

Money: Sri Lanka Rupee = 100 cents

Weather: Tropical, with little change in temperature throughout the year. Heavy monsoon rain falls from May to September.

Main rivers: Mahaweli Ganga, Kelani Ganga

National day: 4 February

National flag: Yellow with two panels. The panel nearest the flagpole has two vertical stripes of green and orange. The other panel is a dark red square on which stands a gold lion holding a sword; in each corner of the square is a gold 'bo' leaf. The dark red part of the flag was the old flag of the former kings of Kandys, who once ruled the island. The green and orange represent the other peoples living on the island.

● The name Sri Lanka means 'Resplendent Land' and comes from a Hindu story.

Sri Lanka

- Sri Lanka elected the world's first woman prime minister when Mrs Sirimavo Bandaranaike won the general election in 1960.

- Adam's Peak, one of the island's highest mountains, is regarded as a holy site by the followers of three religions. Buddhists visit the mountain to see a footprint they believe was made by Buddha. Christians and Moslems make their pilgrimage because there is a tradition that Adam lived here after he was expelled from the Garden of Eden.

- The Temple of the Tooth in Kandy is also an important Buddhist centre. This is the principal Buddhist shrine in Sri Lanka and contains a tooth believed to have come from the mouth of Buddha himself.

- You have to careful where you put your feet in Sri Lanka! More people die here from snake bites (an average of 800 per year) than anywhere else in the world.

- Just under one-third of the farming land in Sri Lanka is used for growing tea, the island's most important crop. A little over a century ago coffee was the main crop until a serious fungus disease killed off almost all the coffee plants. The economy of Sri Lanka would have been ruined had it not been for the successful introduction of tea and rubber.

- All education from nursery school to university is free in Sri Lanka, and around ninety per cent of the population aged ten or over can read and write.

Sudan

Official name: The Republic of the Sudan
History: The Sudan was controlled by Egypt and the UK from the end of the 19th century until 1955 when the country became independent.
World location: North-east Africa, with its coastline on the Red Sea
Area: 2,505,813 km²
Local time: 2 hours ahead of GMT
Population: 23,800,000
Language: Arabic; local languages are also spoken
Religion: Mainly Moslem; smaller Christian community
Capital: Khartoum
Other major centres: Omdurman, Khartoum North, Port Sudan
Money: Sudanese pound = 100 piastres
Weather: Hot and dry in northern desert areas, wet and humid in the south
Main rivers: Nile
Main mountain ranges: Darfur Highlands, Nubian Mountains
National day: 1 January
National flag: Three horizontal stripes of red, white and black with a green triangle next to the flagpole.

- In Arabic Sudan means 'The Country of the Blacks'.
- The Sudan is the largest country in Africa.
- Sudan is the world's leading producer of gum arabic, a substance that is used in the manufacture of perfume and sweets.
- In Sudan there are only thirty-five hours of television broadcast each week and there is less than one television set in the country for every twenty people.

Surinam

Official name: Republic of Surinam
History: For most of its history since the 17th century Surinam had been a Dutch colony. In 1975 it became fully independent.
World location: North-east of South America
Area: 163,265 km^2
Local time: 3 hours behind GMT
Population: 390,000
Language: Dutch, English, Surinamese; Spanish is to be the main working language.
Religion: Hindu, Christian, Moslem
Capital: Paramaribo
Other major centres: Surinam, Nickerjie, Marowijne
Money: Surinam guilder = 100 cents
Weather: Hot and humid with heavy rainfall
Main rivers: Corantijn, Nickerie, Coppename, Saramacca
Main mountain ranges: Wilhelmina Gebergte, Kayser Gebergte
National day: 25 November
National flag: Five horizontal stripes of green, white, red, white, green. The red stripe is twice the width of the green stripes, which are twice as wide as the white ones. In the middle of the red stripe is a gold star.

- Surinam is the home of a very unusual toad that takes its name from the country. Just before she lays her eggs, the back of the female Surinam toad becomes thick and spongy. After laying the eggs, she rolls on to them, so that the eggs sink into her back. About two and half months later the tadpoles are ready to be hatched and work their way out of her skin.
- In the seventeenth century Surinam was swapped by the British for an island and the land around it on the

north-east coast of America. The Dutch who originally owned this area called it New Amsterdam. Today we call it New York.

Swaziland

Official name: Kingdom of Swaziland
History: Swaziland has been a kingdom since the 18th century.
World location: South-east Africa. Except for an eastern border with Mozambique, Swaziland is completely surrounded by South Africa.
Area: 17,363 km^2
Local time: 2 hours ahead of GMT
Population: 740,000
Language: English and Swazi
Religion: Christian; traditional local religions are also followed.
Capital: Mbabane
Other major centres: Manzini, Havelock Mine, Siteki
Money: Lilangeni = 100 cents
Weather: Cool and dry from May to September, hotter and wetter November to March.
Main rivers: Usutu, Komati, Umbuluzi
Main mountain range: Lobombo
National day: 6 September
National flag: Five horizontal stripes of blue, yellow, crimson, yellow, blue. In the centre of the crimson stripe is a black and white African shield laid over two spears and a staff.

● Swaziland is an important producer of asbestos, with one of the world's biggest asbestos mines at Havelock.
● For a small country Swaziland has considerable variation

in height. The country is divided into three areas ranging from 300 metres to 1,200 metres above sea level. Many different plants grow in these varied areas, including over 2,500 flowering plants and ferns.

Sweden

Official name: Kingdom of Sweden
History: Sweden has been an independent country since the 10th century. It became a monarchy in the 19th century.
World location: Northern Europe. Sweden occupies the main part of the Scandinavian peninsula.
Area: 449,964 km^2
Local time: 1 hour ahead of GMT (summer time 2 hours ahead)
Population: 8,440,000
Language: Swedish
Religion: Christian (Lutheran)
Capital: Stockholm
Other major centres: Göteborg, Malmö, Uppsala, Norrköping
Money: Swedish Krona = 100 ore
Weather: Mild, warm summers and long cold winters in the north; milder in the south
Main rivers: Ume, Torne, Angerman, Klar
Main mountain ranges: Norrland Mountains, Smaland Highlands
National day: 6 June
National flag: Blue with a yellow cross.

● The Swedes have one of the highest standards of living in the world. They spend more money per person on holidays than any other nation in Europe.

- Over half of Sweden is covered by forests.
- The name Stockholm means 'Log Island'.
- Cross-country skiing is very popular in Sweden. In March every year the Vasa ski race takes place in which several thousand competitors race over a distance of 89 km.
- St Lucia's Day (13 December) is an important festival in Sweden. Before dawn young girls wake up the household with special wheat cakes and sing a traditional song. At the darkest time of the year they celebrate the coming return of light by wearing crowns of candles.
- There is a town in Sweden named A.

Switzerland

Official name: Swiss Confederation
History: Switzerland has been an independent country since the 17th century.
World location: Central Europe
Area: 41,293 km²
Local time: 1 hour ahead of GMT (summer time 2 hours ahead)
Population: 6,510,000
Language: German, French, Italian and Romansch
Religion: Christian
Capital: Bern
Other major centres: Zürich, Basel, Geneva, Lausanne
Money: Swiss Franc = 100 centimes
Weather: Warm; fairly wet summers and colder, drier winters with heavy snowfalls on the mountains
Main rivers: Rhein (Rhine)/ Aare, Rhône, Inn, Ticino
Main mountain range: Alps
National day: 1 August

Switzerland

National flag: Red, with a white cross.

- More than half of Switzerland is covered by mountains and over a quarter of the country is of no use for agriculture of any sort.
- It was only in 1971 that Swiss women were granted the right to vote in the country's elections and referendums.
- There is no regular army in Switzerland. However, almost all the men go on military training once a year as part of the national defence force. They keep their weapons and uniforms at home and can be called on to help defend their country between the ages of twenty and fifty (fifty-five in the case of officers).
- When the International Red Cross was established in Geneva, it reversed the Swiss flag to form its own flag with a red cross instead of a white cross.
- The national Swiss game is *Hornussen*, which is similar to baseball in that the batter has to hit a ball with a bat. What makes the game unusual is that the fielders try to catch the ball with rackets.

Syria

Official name: Syrian Arab Republic
History: The history of Syria stretches back for over 4,000 years. From the Middle Ages it formed part of the Turkish Ottoman Empire. It was controlled by France between the First and Second World Wars and became independent in 1943.
World location: Middle East, with its western coastline on the Mediterranean Sea.
Area: 185,180 km²
Local time: 2 hours ahead of GMT (summer time 3 hours ahead)

Population: 11,340,000
Language: Arabic
Religion: Moslem
Capital: Damascus
Other major centres: Aleppo, Homs, Lattakia, Hama
Money: Syrian pound = 100 piastres
Weather: Dry, hot summers and mild, wet winters
Main rivers: Al Furat (Euphrates headwaters), Asi (Orontes)
Main mountain ranges: Ansariyah, Jabal ar-Ruwa
National day: 17 April
National flag: Three horizontal stripes of red, white and black, with two green stars on the white stripe.

- The first known alphabet was developed in Syria and artists from Syria had an important influence on the art and architecture of Ancient Greece and Rome.
- Damascus is the oldest capital in the world and the people of Damascus say theirs is also the oldest inhabited city. There have been people living in Damascus since 2500 BC.
- Syrians eat bread as their main food. They also eat dairy products, fresh fruit and vegetables. Lamb dishes are prepared for special occasions.

Taiwan

Official name: Republic of China
History: The island of Taiwan was occupied by Japan from the end of the 19th century until the end of the Second World War. In 1949 it became the headquarters for Chinese Nationalist forces towards the end of their civil war with the Communists on the mainland of China.
World location: Eastern Asia. The island of Taiwan is

Taiwan

about 300 km off the south-east coast of China. Some smaller islands closer to the mainland are also part of Taiwan.

Area: 35,981 km²
Local time: 8 hours ahead of GMT
Population: 19,500,000
Language: Chinese
Religion: Buddhist, Taoist, Christian
Capital: Taipei
Other major centres: Kaohsiung, Taichung, Tainan
Money: New Taiwan Dollar = 100 cents
Weather: Mild winters and rainy summers
Main rivers: Hsia-tan-shui Chi, Choshui Chi, Tan-shui Ho.
Main mountain range: Chunyang Shanmo
National day: 10 October
National flag: Red, with a blue panel in the upper corner next to the flagpole on which is a twelve-pointed white sun.

- The government of Taiwan spends more than one-third of its money each year on defence.
- Half the people of Taiwan depend on farming for their living. The island is also heavily forested, especially in the mountain areas; in fact half of Taiwan is covered with trees.

Tanzania

Official name: United Republic of Tanzania
History: Tanzania was created in 1964 when Tanganyika, which had been a British colony, joined Zanzibar, which had been under British protection.

World location: East central Africa, with its eastern coastline on the Indian Ocean.
Area: 945,087 km²
Local time: 3 hours ahead of GMT
Population: 24,000,000
Language: English is the official language; Kiswahili is the national language.
Religion: Christian, Moslem and traditional tribal religions
Capital: Dodoma
Other major centres: Dar es Salaam, Zanzibar, Mwanza
Money: Tanzanian shilling = 100 cents
Weather: Hot and humid on the coast, drier on the central plateau, cooler in the highlands
Main rivers: Pangani, Rufiji, Rovuma
Main mountain range: Southern Highlands
National day: 26 April
National flag: Two triangles coloured green and blue, divided by a black stripe edged with yellow.

- Tanzania has the world's largest wildlife reserves in the Serengeti Plain and the Ngorongoro Crater.
- Lake Tanganyika is the second largest lake in Africa and the world's second deepest.
- Mount Kilimanjaro lies on the equator close to the Tanzanian border with Kenya. It is the highest mountain in Africa, reaching a height of 5,895 metres, and has snow on its summit all year round. Kilimanjaro is an extinct volcano and stands on its own.

Thailand

Official name: Kingdom of Thailand
History: Until 1939 Thailand was called Siam.
World location: South-east Asia, with its coastline on the Gulf of Siam in the South China Sea
Area: 513,115 km²
Local time: 7 hours ahead of GMT
Population: 54,540,000
Language: Thai
Religion: Mainly Buddhist
Capital: Bangkok
Other major centres: Chiang Mai, Hat Yai, Khon Kaen, Phitsanulok
Money: Baht = 100 satang
Weather: Hot and humid. There are three main seasons: June to October is rainy, November to February is cool, March to May is hot.
Main rivers: Mekong, Chao Pya
National day: 5 December
National flag: Five horizontal stripes of red, white, dark blue, white and red. The dark blue stripe is twice the width of the others.

- The name Thailand means 'Land of the Free'.
- The Tump Nak restaurant in Bangkok is made up to sixty-five houses joined together. The restaurant is staffed by 1,000 waiters.
- The Mekong River is the home of a very rare and very large catfish, the *pa beuk*, which measures 3 metres in length. This is eaten as a special delicacy at Thai feasts.
- Thailand's hog-nosed bat is the world's smallest mammal. It has a wingspan of only 160 mm and weighs about 2 g. It's also known as the Bumblebee bat.

- In Buddhist countries all over the Far East worshippers have built sacred towers called pagodas. The tallest of these is at Nakhon Pathom in Thailand and stands 115 metres high.
- The national sport in Thailand is Thai boxing, in which boxers are allowed to fight with their feet as well as their fists.

Togo

Official name: Togolese Republic
History: Togo was protected by Germany from the 19th century until the First World War. France took control of it in 1914 until 1960, when Togo became fully independent.
World location: West Africa, with southern coastal strip on the Atlantic Ocean
Area: 56,785 km^2
Local time: GMT
Population: 3,250,000
Language: French is the offical language; Ewe and Kabre are also spoken.
Religion: Mainly Christian; smaller Moslem and Hindu communities
Capital: Lomé
Other major centres: Sokodé, Kpalimé, Atakpamé
Money: CFA Franc = 100 centimes
Weather: Hot and humid
National day: 13 January
National flag: Five horizontal stripes of green and yellow. In the upper corner next to the flagpole is a red square with a white star.

Togo

- Only just over a quarter of the people in Togo live in towns.
- There is one television set in Togo to every 250 people.

Tokelau

History: Tokelau became part of New Zealand in 1948.
World location: South-west Pacific Ocean, 430 km north of Western Samoa
Area: 10 km²
Local time: 11 hours behind GMT
Population: 1,700
Language: Tokelauan; English is also spoken.
Religion: Christian
Money: New Zealand dollar
Weather: Tropical, warm all year.

- Two of the islands in Tokelau were severely damaged by tropical storms in 1987 and all the islands were hit by the tidal waves that followed which caused widespread damage.
- There are no roads on Tokelau. Local transport is mainly by boat.

Tonga

Official name: Kindom of Tonga
History: From 1900 until 1970 Tonga was under the protection of the UK.
World location: South-west Pacific Ocean. Tonga

consists of three groups of islands about 3,000 km
north-east of Sydney, Australia
Area: 748 km²
Local time: 13 hours ahead of GMT
Population: 120,000
Language: Tongan, English
Religion: Mainly Christian; smaller Hindu and Moslem
communities
Capital: Nuku'alofa
Money: Tongan pa'anga = 100 seniti
Weather: Warm and comfortable, except from January
to March when the weather is hot and humid
National day: 4 June
National flag: Red, with a white panel in the upper
corner next to the flagpole containing a red cross.

- The British explorer Captain James Cook called Tonga
  'The Friendly Isles' when he visited them in 1773.
- Tonga is the smallest kingdom in the world and the only
  surviving monarchy in the Pacific.

Trinidad and Tobago

Official name: Republic of Trinidad and Tobago
History: Trinidad was occupied by the Spanish and the
French before the British took control of the island in the
19th century. Tobago joined in 1889. The islands
became independent in 1962.
World location: Eastern Caribbean Sea
Area: 5,130 km²
Local time: 4 hours behind GMT
Population: 1,240,000
Language: English

Trinidad and Tobago

Religion: Christian; smaller Hindu and Moslem communities
Capital: Port-of-Spain
Other major centres: San Fernando, Arima
Money: Trinidad and Tobago Dollar = 100 cents
Weather: Tropical with a dry season from January to May
Main rivers: Caroni, Ortoire, Oropuche
Main mountain ranges: Northern and Southern Central
National days: 31 August, 24 September
National flag: Red, with a diagonal black stripe edged in white.

- Musical instruments called *pans* are popular on Trinidad and Tobago. They are precussion instruments made out of empty oil drums. The folk music called Calypso originated in Trinidad.
- Tobago is said to be the island where the adventure story *Robinson Crusoe* is set.
- Vampire bats are found in Trinidad. As blood suckers they can carry the disease rabies and in 1933 over forty people died after being bitten by the vampire bats.
- Pitch Lake in the south-west of Trinidad is filled with asphalt, the substance like tar which is mixed with sand and gravel to make road surfaces. The lake is the world's largest single source of asphalt. You can walk across its surface, but if you stand still, your feet slowly sink into thick sticky asphalt.

Tunisia

Official name: Republic of Tunisia
History: Tunisia was under French protection from 1883 until it became independent in 1956.
World location: North Africa, with its northern coastline on the Mediterranean Sea
Area: 163,610 km^2
Local time: 1 hour ahead of GMT (summer time 2 hours ahead)
Population: 7,810,000
Language: Arabic; French is also spoken
Religion: Mainly Moslem
Capital: Tunis
Other major centres: Sfax, Aryanah, Bizerta
Money: Tunisian dinar = 1,000 millimes
Weather: Hot and dry inland, cooler and wetter on the coast.
Main rivers: Medjerda
National day: 20 March
National flag: Red with a white circle in the middle. In the circle is a red star encircled by a red crescent.

- The ruins of the ancient city of Carthage lie in modern Tunisia. Carthage was once a powerful city-state that challenged the might of Rome. Hannibal, the great Carthaginian leader, invaded Italy by leading an army equipped with elephants over the Alps to defeat many Roman armies
- More than half the population of Tunisians live within 50 km of the coast where the land is fertile. If you go further inland it becomes drier and sandier until there is nothing but bare desert.

Turkey

Official name: Republic of Turkey
History: Turkey was once the centre of the powerful Ottoman Empire. Modern Turkey dates from 1922 following the Turkish War of Independence.
World location: South-east Europe. Turkey has a northern coastline on the Black Sea, a western coastline on the Aegean Sea and a southern coastline on the Mediterranean Sea.
Area: 779,452 km^2
Local time: 2 hours ahead of GMT (summer time 3 hours ahead)
Population: 52,420,000
Language: Turkish
Religion: Moslem
Capital: Ankara
Other major centres: Istanbul, Izmir, Adana, Bursa, Gaziantep, Konya
Money: Turkish Lira = 100 kurus
Weather: The Mediterranean coast has mild winters and warm summers. On the central plateau the summers are hot and dry and the winters cold and snowy.
Main rivers: Firat (Euphrates), Dicle (Tigris), Kizilirmak (Halys)
Main mountain ranges: Armenian Plateau, Taurus Mountains, Anatolian Plateau
National day: 29 October
National flag: Red, with a white crescent and star.

- Turkey has one of the oldest surviving bridges in the world. The bridge spans the Meles River and dates from about 850 BC
- Istanbul lies in two continents, Europe and Asia. Between both parts of the city lies a stretch of sea called the Bosphorus. This may look like a wide river, but it joins

the Black Sea with the Sea of Marmara and separates European and Asian Istanbul.

- Only about one-fifth of the farming land in Turkey is cultivated. The rest is used for pasture.
- The Van cat that gets its name from Lake Van in eastern Turkey is one of the very few cats in the world that likes water and actually enjoys swimming.
- Cracked wheat bread and yoghurt are among the chief foods eaten in Turkey. Turkish cooking has become world famous for its *shish kebab*, which consists of lamb, tomatoes and peppers cooked on a skewer. A popular desert is *baklava*, made of thin layers of pastry, honey and nuts.

Tuvalu

History: From the end of the 19th century until 1978, when it became independent, Tuvalu had been a British colony.

World location: South-west Pacific Ocean. Tuvalu consists of a group of islands about 4,000 km north-east of Australia.

Area: 24 km^2

Local time: 12 hours ahead of GMT

Population: 8,200

Language: Tuvaluan, English

Religion: Mainly Christian

Capital: Funafuti

Money: Australian Dollar = 100 cents

Weather: Warm and comfortable

National day: 1 October

National flag: Light blue with the Union Jack in the upper corner next to the flagpole with nine gold stars arranged in the same pattern as the nine islands.

- *Tuvalu* means 'eight standing together' and refers to the eight inhabited islands that make up the country. The ninth island in the group has no permanent population.
- Nowhere in Tuvalu is higher than 4 metres above sea level. Scientists worry that if the world continues to get warmer and the great icecaps at the North and South Poles melt more and more, then the sea level will rise around the world and low-lying countries like Tuvalu will be flooded and will disappear beneath the waves.

Uganda

Official name: Republic of Uganda
History: Uganda came under British protection in 1894 and became independent in 1962.
World location: East Africa
Area: 236,036 km^2
Local time: 3 hours ahead of GMT
Population: 17,190,000
Language: English is the offical language; Kiswahili is also spoken.
Religion: Mainly Christian
Capital: Kampala
Other major centres: Jinja, Masaka, Mbale, Mbarara
Money: Ugandan New Shilling = 100 cents
Weather: Hot for most of the year, with cool breezes and little variation in temperature.
Main rivers: Nile, Semilki
Main mountain range: Ruwenzori
National day: 9 October
National flag: Six horizontal stripes of black, yellow, red, black, yellow, red. In the centre is a white disc

with the national bird of Uganda, a Baleiric Crested Crane.

- Uganda is the home of another famous bird — Prudle, a grey parrot who is the world's most talkative bird. Prudle has a vocabulary of 800 words.
- The *busuti* is a type of dress worn by women in Uganda and copies a style brought to the country by European missionaries in the 19th century.
- Ninety per cent of the money Uganda earns from other countries comes from selling coffee.
- Uganda has the world's most aggressive butterfly, *Charaxes candiope*, which divebombs anyone who disturbs it.
- Lake Victoria, the largest lake in Africa, covers part of south-east Uganda. This is also the second largest fresh-water lake in the world, covering an area of 69,485 km^2 over three times the size of Wales.

USSR

Official name: Union of Soviet Socialist Republics
History: Until 1917 most of the USSR was known as the Russian Empire governed by the Tsar. In 1917 the Russian Revolution broke out and in 1918 the empire became a Communist republic. In the late 1980s great reforms took place in Soviet life. The government became more open and ordinary people were given greater freedom in their own lives and in their choice of political leaders. These changes in the USSR encouraged similar moves towards greater openness and freedom in several other countries in Eastern Europe.
World location: Eastern Europe and northern Asia. The

USSR

USSR is the largest country in the world and occupies the whole of the north of the continent of Asia as well as much of eastern Europe.

Area: 22,402,200 km^2

Local time: As the USSR covers such a huge area it stretches over several time zones. Moscow and west of the USSR are 3 hours ahead of GMT (summer time 4 hours ahead). The easternmost areas are 12 hours ahead of GMT (summer time 13 hours ahead).

Population: 283,680,000

Language: Russian; local languages are also spoken

Religion: Mainly Russian Orthodox; smaller Moslem, Christian and Jewish communities.

Capital: Moscow

Other major centres: Leningrad, Kiev, Tashkent, Baku, Kharkov, Minsk

Money: Rouble = 100 kopecks

Weather: Great variation. Central Asia is very hot in summer, north-east Siberia is very cold in winter. In Moscow the summers are short and hot, the winters long and cold.

Main rivers: The USSR has some of the longest rivers in the world (14 are over 1,600 km long). In Europe some of them are the Volga, the Ural, the Dnieper and the Don. Some of the Asian ones are the Ob, the Yenisei, the Lena and the Amur.

Main mountain ranges: Caucasus, Urals, Pamirs, Tien Shan

National Day: 7 November

National flag: Red, with a gold hammer and sickle below a gold star in the upper corner next to the flagpole.

- The USSR has a larger number of people in its armed forces than any other country on earth.
- The Soviet spacecraft *Sputnik 1* became the first

spacecraft to circle the earth when it went into orbit in 1957. The word *sputnik* means 'fellow traveller'.

- The USSR has the world's largest art gallery in the Winter Palace and neighbouring Hermitage in Leningrad. There are more than 3,000,000 items in its collection.
- Siberia in the eastern area of the USSR contains one quarter of the forests on earth.
- Siberia also contains the world's deepest lake. Lake Baikal is so deep that experts calculate it contains 23,000 km^3 of water.
- Moscow's Hotel Rossiya has 3,200 rooms.
- In 1987 there were 1,202,000 doctors and dentists in the USSR. That's one to every 236 people, more doctors and dentists per head than any other country.

United Arab Emirates

History: The United Arab Emirates are seven small states that were under British protection from the 19th century until 1971.

World location: Middle East, with its northern coastline on the Persian Gulf

Area: 83,657 km^2

Local time: 4 hours ahead of GMT

Population: 1,500,000

Language: Arabic

Religion: Moslem

Capital: Abu Dhabi

Other major centres: Dubai, Sharjah, Ras al-Khaimah

Money: UAE Dirham = 100 fils

Weather: Very hot and humid

Main mountain range: Al-Hajar

National day: 2 December

United Arab Emirates

National flag: Three horizontal stripes of green, white and black, with a vertical red stripe next to the flagpole.

- At one time the coast of the United Arab Emirates was rightly known as the Pirate Coast, because of the number of merchant ships that were attacked by pirates hiding in the inlets along it.
- The discovery of oil has brought great wealth to the United Arab Emirates. Today the country has the second highest income per person in the world.

United Kingdom

Official name: United Kingdom of Great Britain and Northern Ireland
History: The United Kingdom was established at the beginning of the 19th century when Great Britain and Ireland were legally joined.
World location: North-west Europe. The UK is made up of the island of Great Britain, the north-east part of the island of Ireland and a number of surrounding islands.
Area: 244,100 km^2
Local time: GMT (summer time 1 hour ahead of GMT)
Population: 57,080,000
Language: English; Welsh and Gaelic are spoken in certain areas.
Religion: Christian; smaller Moslem, Hindu, Sikh and Jewish communities
Capital: London
Other major centres: Birmingham, Glasgow, Leeds, Sheffield, Liverpool, Bradford, Manchester, Edinburgh, Bristol
Money: Pound = 100 pence

Weather: Cool summers and mild winters, colder in northern mountain areas.

Main rivers: Severn, Thames, Trent, Aire/ Ouse/ Humber, Great Ouse, Wye, Tay.

Main mountain ranges: Grampians, North-west Highlands, Cairngorms, Snowdonia

National days: 1 March, 17 March, 23 April, 30 November

National flag: Union Jack.

- The British monarchy is over 1,000 years old. Queen Elizabeth II is descended from the earliest kings of England.
- The largest library in the United Kingdom, the British Library, has a collection of over 8,000,000 books.
- Hamleys in Regent Street, London, is the world's biggest toy shop, with six floors filled with toys.
- The Ashmolean Museum in Oxford is the world's longest surviving museum.
- The Faversham Oyster Fishery Company is the world's oldest company. It has been in business since the 12th century.
- The Queen's home at Windsor Castle is the largest inhabited castle in the world.
- Fifty years ago London was the world's largest city. Today it isn't even in the top ten.

United States of America

History: Until 1776 the original thirteen states of the American Union were British colonies. On 4 July 1776 they declared themselves independent. There are now fifty states.

World location: North America. The USA is the fourth largest country in the world, with its coastline on the Pacific Ocean and eastern coastline on the Atlantic Ocean.

Area: 9,363,123 km²

Local time: The USA stretches across several time zones: Eastern time is 5 hours behind GMT, Central time is 6 hours behind GMT, Mountain time is 7 hours behind GMT, Pacific Time is 8 hours behind GMT, Alaska is 9 hours behind GMT, Hawaii is 10 hours behind GMT.

Population: 246,330,000

Language: English; other European languages, especially Spanish, are also spoken

Religion: Mainly Christian; smaller Jewish community

Capital: Washington D.C.

Other major centres: New York, Chicago, Los Angeles, Philadelphia, Houston, Detroit, Dallas, San Diego, Phoenix, Baltimore

Money: US Dollar = 100 cents

Weather: Great variation from hot and humid in the south to very cold in Alaska. Milder on the coasts than in the interior, where summers are hot and winters very cold.

Main rivers: Mississippi-Missouri, Arkansas, Colorado, Ohio Columbia, Red, Rio Grande

Main mountain ranges: Rocky Mountains, Appalachian Mountains, Alaska Range, Cascade Range

National day: 4 July

National flag: Stars and Stripes, with seven red stripes and six white, representing the original 13 states in the Union. There are 50 stars, one for each of the present states.

- Many important inventions have taken place in America, among which are: the development of the polio vaccine, the electric lightbulb, the zip fastener, the telephone, the electric washing-machine, nylon, the microprocessor and the aeroplane.

- Coca-Cola, another American discovery, is the world's most popular soft drink. Over 301,000,000 Coca-Colas are sold around the world every day.

- There are 8,500 public libraries in the USA.

- About 98 per cent of all American homes have at least one television set. On average the set is switched on for about six hours a day.

- The Sears Roebuck Tower in Chicago is the world's tallest inhabited building, rising to a height of 443 metres.

- The USA is also the home of two distinctive types of music – Jazz and Rock 'n' Roll.

- In Death Valley in California less than 5 cm of rain falls every year. Death Valley also recorded the highest temperature ever in the USA when the thermometer read 57° C.

- Out of every 100 cars in the world 38 are to be found in the USA.

- There's a Bristlecone pine tree growing on the side of the White Mountains in California which experts calculate is 4,600 years old and the oldest living tree in the world.

- The Niagara Falls that lie between Lake Ontario and Lake Erie are slowly moving backwards. Scientists have noticed that the rushing water is slowly wearing away the rocks over which the falls run and they estimate that in about 25,000 years time the falls will have worked their way back to Lake Erie and may disappear altogether.

Uruguay

Official name: Oriental Republic of Uruguay
History: Uruguay was a Spanish colony from the early 18th century until it became fully independent in 1828.
World location: East central South America, with its eastern coastline on the South Atlantic Ocean.
Area: 176,215 km^2
Local time: 3 hours behind GMT (December to February 2 hours behind)
Population: 3,060,000
Language: Spanish
Religion: Christian (mainly Roman Catholic)
Capital: Montevideo
Other major centres: Salto, Paysandu, Las Piedras
Money: New peso = 100 centesimos
Weather: Warm summers and mild winters
Main river: Uruguay
National day: 25 August
National flag: Nine horizontal stripes of white and blue. In the upper corner next to the flagpole is a white panel on which is a gold sun with a face.

- Ninety per cent of the land in Uruguay is given over to farming and ninety per cent of that is used for raising livestock, mainly cattle and sheep. Thirty-five per cent of the country's earnings from other countries come from animals and animal products.

Vanuatu

Official name: Republic of Vanuatu

History: For most of this century Vanuatu was governed by the UK and France under the name of the New Hebrides. The islands became independent in 1980.

World location: South-west Pacific Ocean. Vanuatu consists of 12 main islands and about 50 smaller ones about 800 km west of Fiji

Area: 14,763 km^2

Local time: 12 hours ahead of GMT (December to February 11 hours ahead)

Population: 150,000

Language: English and French are the official languages; local languages, especially Bislama, are also spoken

Religion: Mainly Christian

Capital: Vila

Money: Vatu = 100 centimes

Weather: Warm and comfortable for most of the year

National day: 30 July

National flag: Two horizontal stripes of red and green, separated by a thinner black stripe. On the side next to the flagpole is a black triangle that runs into the black stripe and lying in the whole black area is a thin yellow stripe shaped like the letter 'Y' on its side. In the black triangle is the tusk of a wild boar with two fern leaves crossed over it.

- Over the next twenty years there are plans to plant 10,000 trees on Vanuatu to replace those cut down for fuel and building timber.
- Copra, the dried insides of coconuts, provides over sixty per cent of Vanuatu's foreign earnings.
- Since the UK and France used to govern Vanuatu jointly, both French and English primary schools were

created. In 1987 there were 224 English primary schools and 105 French ones; however the French schools each had more pupils.

Vatican

Official name: State of the Vatican City
History: For hundreds of years the Popes governed a large part of Italy. In the 19th century most of their territory was taken into the Kingdom of Italy. Today the Vatican City is still an independent state.
World location: Southern Europe. The Vatican lies within the city of Rome. It is the smallest country in the world.
Area: 0.44 km²
Local time: 1 hour ahead of GMT (summer time 2 hours ahead)
Population: 1,000
Language: Italian
Religion: Christian (Roman Catholic)
Money: Lira = 100 centesimi
Weather: Hot summers, mild winters
National day: 22 October
National flag: Two vertical stripes of yellow and white. On the white stripe are the crossed keys and triple crown, the Pope's emblem.

- The Vatican is guarded by a force of Swiss soldiers that are still dressed in 16th century uniforms when they are on duty. These uniforms are said to have been designed by the great painter Michelangelo.
- In spite of being the smallest country in the world the Vatican is the third most crowded.
- The Vatican has the lowest birth rate in the world − nil.

Most of the people living there are Catholic priests who are not allowed to marry.

Venezuela

Official name: Republic of Venezuela
History: Venezuela was a Spanish colony until it became independent in 1821.
World location: North of South America
Area: 912,050 km²
Local time: 4 hours behind GMT
Population: 18,750,000
Language: Spanish
Religion: Christian (Roman Catholic)
Capital: Caracas
Other major centres: Maracaibo, Valencia, Barquisimeto
Money: Boloivar = 100 centimos
Weather: Hot and humid in the lowlands, cooler in the highlands
Main river: Orinoco
Main mountain ranges: Cordillera de Merida, Sierra de Perija, La Gran Sabana
National day: 5 July
National flag: Three horizontal stripes of yellow, blue and red. In the centre of the blue stripe is an arc of seven white stars and the country's coat of arms appears in the upper corner next to the flagpole.

- The early explorers of Venezuela were reminded of the Italian city of Venice and named their new discovery 'Little Venice', or Venezuela, after it.
- The Venezuelan national dish is called the *hallaca*. This is made of dough filled with meat and cooked in

wrappers made of banana leaves. It is often served at Christmas.

- Jesus is a popular first name in Venezuela.
- The national folk dance is the *joropo*. It's a dance in which you stamp your feet in time to the music played on guitars, harps and rattles called maracas.
- There's a motorway in Venezuela called the *arana*, 'the spider'.
- Venezuela has the world's highest waterfall, the Angel Falls, over which water plunges 979 metres from top to bottom.

Vietnam

Official name: Socialist Republic of Vietnam
History: For much of its history Vietnam was controlled by China. In the 19th century the country became a French colony. Japan occupied Vietnam during the Second World War. In 1954 the country was split into North Vietnam and South Vietnam following fighting with France. Further fighting, involving the USA, lasted from 1961 until 1973. Vietnam became a single country once again, under a Communist government, in 1976.
World location: South-east Asia, with its eastern and southern coastlines on the South China sea.
Area: 329,556 km^2
Local time: 7 hours ahead of GMT
Population: 64,230,000
Language: Vietnamese
Religion: Buddhism, Taoism
Capital: Hanoi
Other major centres: Ho Chi Minh City, Haiphong, Da-nhang
Money: Dong = 100 hao

Weather: Warm and humid in the south, hot and wet in the north
Main rivers: Mekong, Songkoi, Songko
National day: 2 September
National flag: Red, with a yellow star in the centre.

- In the Annamese language the name Vietnam means 'Land of the South'.
- Many families in Vietnam live together in what are known as extended families. These usually consist of the parents, the unmarried children and the oldest married son and his family.

Virgin Islands, British

Official name: Colony of British Virgin Islands
History: The Virgin Islands have been a British colony since the 17th century.
World location: Eastern Caribbean Sea, group of islands to the east of Cuba.
Area: 153 km²
Local time: 4 hours behind GMT
Population: 12,100
Language: English
Religion: Christian
Capital: Road Town
Money: US Dollar = 100 cents.
Weather: Warm, comfortable climate with sea breezes to prevent it becoming too hot
National flag: British Blue Ensign with the coat of arms of the British Virgin Islands.

- The Virgin Islands provided the setting for Robert Louis Stevenson's adventure story *Treasure Island*.

- The islands were used by pirates for many years and they gave some of the islands colourful names like Dead Man's Chest, Little Dogs and Prickly Pear.

Western Samoa

Official name: The Independent State of Western Samoa

History: From the end of the 19th century until the First World War Western Samoa was governed by Germany. From 1920 until 1961 New Zealand took control. Western Samoa became independent in 1962.

World location: South central Pacific Ocean. There are nine islands in the Samoan group. New Zealand is about 2,900 km to the south-west.

Area: 2,831 km^2

Local time: 11 hours behind GMT

Population: 170,000

Language: Samoan, English

Religion: Christian

Capital: Apia

Money: Western Samoan tala = 100 sene

Weather: Warm most of the year, slightly cooler from May to September

National day: 1 January

National flag: Red, with a blue panel in the upper corner next to the flagpole in which there are five white stars representing the Southern Cross, a group of stars only seen below the Equator.

- Western Samoa consists of a chain of volcanic islands, with many streams and waterfalls providing the power to produce most the country's hydro-electricity.

- The Polynesian people on Western Samoa have been living on the islands for at least 2,000 years.
- During its early history Western Samoa was ruled by several different chiefs and there was a lot of fighting between them. The country was finally united in the 16th century by a woman called Salamasina.
- Robert Louis Stevenson, the author of *Treasure Island*, lived on Western Samoa for several years and is buried on one of the islands.
- The smallest spider ever found was discovered in Western Samoa. It measured 0.43 mm, making it smaller than the head of a needle.

Yemen

Official name: The Republic of Yemen
History: In May 1990 the Republic of Yemen was created out of two neighbouring countries: the Yemen Arab Republic (North Yemen) and the People's Democratic Republic of Yemen (South Yemen). South Yemen had been a British territory in the 19th century and had become independent in 1967. North Yemen had been a monarchy ruled by an Iman until 1962, when a republic was proclaimed.
World location: Middle East — Yemen is in the south-west corner of the Arabian peninsula with a western coastline on the Red Sea and a southern coastline on the Arabian Sea.
Area: 531,869 km^2
Local time: 3 hours ahead of GMT
Population: 10,040,000
Language: Arabic
Religion: Moslem
Capital: San'a

Yemen

Other major centres: Aden, Hodeida, Ta'iz, Ibb, Mukalla
Money: Yemen rial = 100 fils
Weather: Very hot and humid on the coast, cooler in the highlands inland.
Main mountain range: Yemen Highlands
National day: 22 May, 26 September, 14 October
National flag: Three horizontal stripes of red, white and black.

- Yemen gets its name from the Arabic word *Al Yaman* which means 'Land on the right hand'. This was how the ancient geographers of the holy city of Mecca used to describe South Arabia.
- The northern part of Yemen is the most fertile and cultivated area of the whole Arabian peninsula.
- Rice, bread, lamb and fish are the main foods of the Yemeni. However, the country's desert people live on bread and ilb nuts, which they gather from thorn trees.
- Clothing in the Yemen is often white because this deflects the heat of the sun. The men often wear white silk robes, turbans and leather sandals. The women wear long robes and shawls or veils over their heads.
- The Yemen is famous for its Mocha coffee, named after the port from where it was first shipped to other countries.
- In ancient times incense like frankincense and myrrh were grown in the Yemen. It may have been here that the gifts taken by the Three Wise Men to Jesus as a baby originated.
- Yemen once formed part of the Kingdom of Sheba, a rich country which traded with many parts of the Middle East and countries as far away as India. Sheba is mentioned in the Bible and the Old Testament records a visit made by the Queen of Sheba to the court of King Solomon when he was king of Israel. She arrived at the court at the head of a camel caravan carrying precious stones, gold and spices for King Solomon.

- Finding and storing water has concerned the people of Yemen for thousands of years. Although the country receives more rain than any other part of Arabia, there are no permanent streams in the country. Wells are sunk in dry river beds to draw the water that lies underground and dams are built to collect water in the highland regions. Two and a half thousand years ago the people of ancient Sheba built a huge dam to provide water for their capital Ma'rib. Although the dam was destroyed in the 6th century BC, its ruins can still be seen one hundred kilometres north-east of the present-day capital, San'a.

- One advantage of the hot Arabian sun is that it does allow Yemenis to make salt from seawater, which is collected in large shallow containers and then left to evaporate. As the water dries away it leaves the salt behind.

Yugoslavia

Official name: Socialist Federal Republic of Yugoslavia
History: Until 1917 Yugoslavia consisted of a number of independent states. In 1918 these joined together in one kingdom. During the Second World War the country was invaded by Germany and Italy. In 1945, when the war had ended, the country became a republic with a Communist government.
World location: South-east Europe, with its western coastline on the Adriatic Sea
Area: 255,804 km²
Local time: 1 hour ahead of GMT (summer time 2 hours ahead)
Population: 23,560,000
Language: Serbo-Croat, Slovene, Macedonian; Hungarian and Albanian are also spoken.

Yugoslavia

Religion: Christian; smaller community of Moslems
Capital: Belgrade
Other major centres: Zagreb, Skopje, Sarajevo, Ljubljana, Novi Stad
Money: Yugoslav dinar = 100 paras
Weather: Dry, warm summers, with mild, damp winters on the coast; colder winters inland
Main rivers: Dunav (Danube) and tributaries, Vardar
Main mountain ranges: Slovene Alps, Dinaric Mountains, Carpathian and Balkan Mountains
National day: 29 November
National flag: Three horizontal strips of blue, white and red. In the middle of the white stripe is a red star edged with yellow.

- The world's largest tapestry was woven in Yugoslavia. Called the *History of Irak*; it measures 1242.1 sq. metres. You can see it on the wall of an amphitheatre in the capital of Iraq, Baghdad.
- Matej Gaspar, who was born on 11 July 1987, was named the world's five billionth member of the United Nations.
- In the evening many Yugoslavs enjoy the old custom called the *korzo*, which involves strolling along the streets, stopping to chat with friends and just enjoying the evening air.

Zaire

Official name: Republic of Zaire
History: Zaire was a Belgian colony from the end of the 19th century until 1960, when it became independent.
World location: Central Africa, with a short western coastline on the Atlantic Ocean

Area: 2,344,885 km²
Local time: Zaire crosses two time zones: western area 1 hour ahead of GMT, eastern area 2 hours ahead of GMT
Population: 33,460,000
Language: French is the offical language; many local languages are also spoken, in particular Lingala.
Religion: Mainly Christian; smaller Moslem community
Capital: Kinshasa
Other major centres: Lubumbashi, Kisangani, Likasi
Money: Zaire = 100 makuta
Weather: Hot and humid in lowlands, cooler in highlands
Main rivers: Zaire (Congo), Ubangi, Kasai
Main mountain ranges: Chaine des Mitumba, Ruwenzori
National day: 24 November
National flag: Green, in the middle of which is a yellow disc with an arm holding a flaming torch.

- Corn and rice are important parts of the diet in Zaire. Often food is served as a thick porridge with a spicy sauce. Fish or meat are added when they are available.
- There are a number of races of very small people called pigmies, living in Zaire. The smallest of these are the Mbuti, whose men have an average height of 137 cm and whose women are about 5 cm shorter.

Zambia

Official name: Republic of Zambia
History: Zambia came under British rule at the end of the 19th century.
World location: South central Africa

Zambia

Area: 752,614 km^2
Local time: 2 hours ahead of GMT
Population: 7,530,000
Language: English; local languages are also spoken.
Religion: Christian; smaller Moslem community
Capital: Lusaka
Other major centres: Kitwe, Ndola, Mufulira
Money: Kwacha ngwee
Weather: September to November is the hot season,
the rainy season lasts from November to April and the
cool season (in which frosts can happen in higher areas)
lasts from May to August.
Main rivers: Zambezi and its tributaries, Luapula
Main mountain range: Muchinga Mountains
National day: 24 October
National flag: Green, with three vertical stripes in the
lower corner opposite the flagpole. The stripes are
coloured dark red, black and orange. Above them flies a
gold eagle.

- Zambia has 18 national parks occupying 60,000 sq. km,
  or 8 per cent of the country.
- Zambia is the world's leading producer of copper, and
  copper provides almost ninety per cent of the country's
  earnings from foreign countries.

Zimbabwe

History: Zimbabwe became a British territory in the 19th
century, when it was then called Rhodesia. It became
independent under its new name in 1980.
World location: South central Africa
Area: 390,580 km^2
Local time: 2 hours ahead of GMT

Population: 8,880,000
Language: English; local languages also spoken
Religion: Christian
Capital: Harare
Other major centres: Bulawayo, Chitungwiza, Gwelo
Money: Zimbabwe dollar = 100 cents
Weather: Warm, with low humidity thanks to its altitude
Main rivers: Zambezi and tributaries, Limpopo and tributaries, Sabi and tributaries.
Main mountain ranges: Enyanga, Melsetter
National day: 15 April
National flag: Seven horizontal stripes of green, yellow, red, black, red, yellow and green. Next to the flagpole is a white triangle edged with black on which is a red star. The Zimbabwe Bird in yellow sits on the star.

- The name Zimbabwe means 'Stone Houses', and the country is named after the ruins of Great Zimabawe which date back to the Middle Ages. The city was once part of a great civilization in this part of southern Africa, and the ruins are the most substantial stone buildings found in Africa south of the Sahara.
- Nearly one-fifth of the world's tobacco is grown in Zimbabwe. Tobacco is the country's main export.
- The world's largest herds of elephants and buffaloes live in Zimbabwe.

Other great reads *from* **Red Fox**

Further Red Fox titles that you might enjoy reading are listed on the following pages. They are available in bookshops or they can be ordered directly from us.

If you would like to order books, please send this form and the money due to:

ARROW BOOKS, BOOKSERVICE BY POST, PO BOX 29, DOUGLAS, ISLE OF MAN, BRITISH ISLES. Please enclose a cheque or postal order made out to Arrow Books Ltd for the amount due, plus 22p per book for postage and packing, both for orders within the UK and for overseas orders.

NAME _____

ADDRESS _____

_____

Please print clearly.

Whilst every effort is made to keep prices low, it is sometimes necessary to increase cover prices at short notice. If you are ordering books by post, to save delay it is advisable to phone to confirm the correct price. The number to ring is THE SALES DEPARTMENT 071 (if outside London) 973 9700.

*Other great reads from **Red Fox***

AMAZING ORIGAMI FOR CHILDREN
Steve and Megumi Biddle

Origami is an exciting and easy way to make toys, decorations and all kinds of useful things from folded paper.

Use leftover gift paper to make a party hat and a fancy box. Or create a colourful lorry, a pretty rose and a zoo full of origami animals. There are over 50 fun projects in Amazing Origami.

Following Steve and Megumi's step-by-step instructions and clear drawings, you'll amaze your friends and family with your magical paper creations.

ISBN 0 09 9661802   £4.99

MAGICAL STRING   Steve and Megumi Biddle

With only a loop of string you can make all kinds of shapes, puzzles and games. Steve and Megumi Biddle provide all the instructions and diagrams that are needed to create their amazing string magic in another of their inventive and absorbing books.

ISBN 0 09 964470 3   £2.50

Other great reads ⌘ *from* **Red Fox**

CRAZY PAINTING Juliet Bawden

There are loads of imaginative ideas and suggstions in this easy-to-follow activity book all about painting. First it teaches you the basics: how to make your own vegetable dyes, mix paints, create a fabulous marbled effect and decorate ceramics. Then the fun begins. You can design your own curtains, make zany brooches for your friends, create your own colourful wrapping paper and amaze your family with hours of painting pleasure.

ISBN 0 09 954320 6 £2.25

DRESSING UP FUN Terry Burrows

Dressing up is always fun—for a party, a play or just for a laugh! In Dressing Up Fun you'll find loads of ideas for all kinds of costumes and make-up. So whether you'd like to be a cowboy, punk or witch, superman, a princess or the Empire State Building, youll find them all in this book.

ISBN 0 09 965110 6 £2.99

Other great reads ✦ *from* **Red Fox**

CRAZY PRESENTS   Juliet Bawden

Would you like to make: Pebble paper weights? Green tomato chutney? Scented hand cream? Patchwork clowns? Leather ties?

By following the step-by-step instructions in this book you can make a huge variety of gifts—from rattles for the very young to footwarmers for the very old. Some cost a few pence, others a little more but all are extra special presents.

ISBN 0 09 967080 1   £2.50

CRAZY PAPER   Eric Kenneway

Origami—the Japanese art of paper folding—is easy and fun to do. You can make boats that float, wriggling snakes, tumbling acrobats, jumping frogs and many more fantastic creatures.

There are easy to follow instructions and clear diagrams in this classic guide used by Japanese schoolchildren.

ISBN 0 09 951380 3   £1.95

Other great reads from **Red Fox**

The Millennium books are novels for older readers from the very best science fiction and fantasy writers

---

A DARK TRAVELLING   Roger Zelazny

An 'ordinary' 14-year-old, James Wiley has lost his father to a parallel world in the darkbands. With the help of his sister Becky, James, the exchange student and Uncle George, the werewolf, James goes in search of his parent.

ISBN 0 09 960970 3   £2.99

PROJECT PENDULUM   Robert Silverberg

Identical twins Sean and Eric have been chosen for a daring experiment. One of them will travel into the distant past. The other into the distant future. And with each swing of the time pendulum they will be further apart . . .

ISBN 0 09 962460 5   £2.99

THE LEGACY OF LEHR   Katherine Kurtz

The interstellar cruiser *Valkyrie* is forced to pick up four sinister, exotic cats, much to the captain's misgivings. His doubts appear justified when a spate of vicious murders appear on board.

ISBN 0 09 960960 6   £2.99

CHESS WITH A DRAGON   David Gerrold

The Galactic InterChange was the greatest discovery in history . . . but now it had brought disaster. Unless Yake could negotiate a deal with the alien in front of him, mankind would be reduced to a race of slaves.

ISBN 0 09 960950 9   £2.99

Other great reads ✎ *from Red Fox*

Fantasy fiction—the Song of the Lioness series

ALANNA—THE FIRST ADVENTURE
Tamora Pierce

Alanna has just one wish—to become a knight. Her twin brother, Thom, prefers magic and wants to be a great sorcerer. So they swop places and Alanna, dressed as a boy, sets off for the king's court. Becoming a knight is difficult—but Alanna is brave and determined to succeed. And her gift for magic is to prove essential to her survival . . .

ISBN 0 09 943560 8 £2.50

IN THE HAND OF THE GODDESS
Tamora Pierce

Alan of Trebond is the smallest but toughest of the squires at court. Only Prince Jonathan knows she is really a girl called Alanna.

As she prepares for her final training to become a knight, Alanna is troubled. Is she the only one to sense the evil in Duke Roger? Does no one realise what a threat his steely ambition poses?

Alanna must use every ounce of her warrior skills and her gift for magic if she is to survive her Ordeal of Knighthood—and outwit the dangerous sorcerer duke.

ISBN 0 09 955560 3 £2.50

The third title in the Song of the Lioness series, THE GIRL WHO RIDES LIKE A MAN will be published by Red Fox in May 1991.

Other great reads from **Red Fox**

THE WINTER VISITOR   Joan Lingard

Strangers didn't come to Nick Murray's home town in winter.
And they didn't lodge at his house. But Ed Black had—and Nick
Murray didn't like it.

Why had Ed come? The small Scottish seaside resort was
bleak, cold and grey at that time of year. The answer, Nick
begins to suspect, lies with his mother—was there some past
connection between her and Ed?

ISBN 0 09 938590 2   £1.99

STRANGERS IN THE HOUSE   Joan Lingard

Calum resents his mother remarrying. He doesn't want to move
to a flat in Edinburgh with a new father and a thirteen-year-old
stepsister. Stella, too, dreads the new marriage. Used to living
alone with her father she loathes the idea of sharing their small
flat.

Stella's and Calum's struggles to adapt to a new life, while
trying to cope with the problems of growing up are related with
great poignancy in a book which will be enjoyed by all older
readers.

ISBN 0 09 955020 2   £1.95

Other great reads from **Red Fox**

Discover the great animal stories of Colin Dann

JUST NUFFIN

The Summer holidays loomed ahead with nothing to look forward to except one dreary week in a caravan with only Mum and Dad for company. Roger was sure he'd be bored.

But then Dad finds Nuffin: an abandoned puppy who's more a bundle of skin and bones than a dog. Roger's holiday is transformed and he and Nuffin are inseparable. But Dad is adamant that Nuffin must find a new home. Is there *any* way Roger can persuade him to change his mind?

ISBN 0 09 966900 5   £1.99

KING OF THE VAGABONDS

'You're very young,' Sammy's mother said, 'so heed my advice. Don't go into Quartermile Field.'

His mother and sister are happily domesticated but Sammy, the tabby cat, feels different. They are content with their lot, never wondering what lies beyond their immediate surroundings. But Sammy is burningly curious and his life seems full of mysteries. Who is his father? Where has he gone? And what is the mystery of Quartermile Field?

ISBN 0 09 957190 0   £2.50

Other great reads ✦ *from Red Fox*

THE SNIFF STORIES   Ian Whybrow

Things just keep happening to Ben Moore. It's dead hard
avoiding disaster when you've got to keep your street cred with
your mates *and* cope with a family of oddballs at the same time.
There's his appalling 2½ year old sister, his scatty parents who
are into healthy eating and animal rights and, worse than all
of these, there's Sniff! If only Ben could just get on with his
scientific experiments and his attempt at a world beating
Swampbeast score . . . but there's no chance of that while chaos
is just around the corner.

ISBN 0 09 9750406   £2.50

J.B. SUPERSLEUTH   Joan Davenport

James Bond is a small thirteen-year-old with spots and
spectacles. But with a name like that, how can he help being
a supersleuth?

It all started when James and 'Polly' (Paul) Perkins spotted
a teacher's stolen car. After that, more and more mysteries
needed solving. With the case of the Arabian prince, the
Murdered Model, the Bonfire Night Murder and the Lost
Umbrella, JB's reputation at Moorside Comprehensive soars.

But some of the cases aren't quite what they seem . . .

ISBN 0 09 9717808   £1.99